The Tempest

William Shakespeare

THE EMC MASTERPIECE SERIES

Access Editions

SERIES EDITOR
Robert D. Shepherd

EMC/Paradigm Publishing
St. Paul, Minnesota

Staff Credits:

For **EMC/Paradigm Publishing**, St. Paul, Minnesota

Laurie Skiba
Editor

Eileen Slater
Editorial Consultant

Shannon O'Donnell Taylor
Associate Editor

Jennifer J. Anderson
Assistant Editor

For **Penobscot School Publishing, Inc.**, Danvers, Massachusetts

Editorial

Robert D. Shepherd
President, Executive Editor

Christina E. Kolb
Managing Editor

Sara Hyry
Editor

Laurie Faria
Associate Editor

Sharon Salinger
Copyeditor

Marilyn Murphy Shepherd
Editorial Advisor

Design and Production

Charles Q. Bent
Production Manager

Sara Day
Art Director

Diane Castro
Compositor

Janet Stebbings
Compositor

ISBN 0-8219-1619-X

Published by EMC/Paradigm Publishing
875 Montreal Way
St. Paul, Minnesota 55102

Printed in the United States of America.
10 9 8 7 6 5 4 3 2 1 xxx 02 01 99 98 97

Table of Contents

William Shakespeare

William Shakespeare

William Shakespeare (1564–1616). William Shakespeare may well be the greatest dramatist the world has ever known. His mother, Mary Arden Shakespeare, was from a well-to-do, well-connected family. His father, John Shakespeare, was a prosperous glove maker and local politician. William's exact birthdate is unknown, but he was baptized in his hometown of Stratford-upon-Avon on April 26, 1564, and tradition has assigned him a birthdate of April 23, which was also the day of his death and the feast day of Saint George, England's patron saint.

Shakespeare attended the Stratford grammar school, where he studied Latin and perhaps some Greek. At the age of eighteen, Shakespeare married an older woman, Anne Hathaway, who was with child. Altogether, William and Anne had three children, Susanna and the twins Hamnet and Judith. He may have worked for a while as a schoolteacher, for there are many references to teaching in his plays. By 1592, however, he was living in London and pursuing a life in the theater. Shakespeare continued to provide for his family and to expand his holdings in Stratford while living in London. He retired to Stratford-upon-Avon at the end of his life.

Shakespeare's Professional Career

By 1593, Shakespeare was a successful actor and playwright. His history plays *Henry the Sixth*, Parts 1, 2, and 3, and *The Tragedy of Richard the Third* had established him as a significant force in London theater. In 1593, when an outbreak of the plague forced the closing of the theaters, Shakespeare turned to narrative poetry, producing *Venus and Adonis* followed by *The Rape of Lucrece*, both dedicated to a patron, the Earl of Southampton. When the theaters reopened, Shakespeare plunged back into his primary vocation, and wrote thirty-seven plays in less than twenty years, including *The Taming of the Shrew; A Midsummer Night's Dream; The Merchant of Venice; Twelfth Night, or What You Will; All's Well That Ends Well; The Tragedy of King Richard the Second; The Tragedy of Romeo and Juliet; The Tragedy of Julius Cæsar; The Tragedy of Hamlet, Prince of Denmark; The Tragedy of Othello, the Moor of Venice; The Tragedy of King Lear; The Tragedy of Macbeth; The Winter's Tale;* and *The Tempest.*

Shakespeare became a shareholder with Richard Burbage, son of John Burbage, in a theater company known as The Lord Chamberlain's Men. In 1599, Burbage, Shakespeare, and others opened the Globe Theater, and in 1603 they bought the Blackfriars, a small, artificially lighted indoor theater for winter performances. Their company began performing regularly at the court of Queen Elizabeth I. After the death of Elizabeth in 1603, Shakespeare's company became, officially, servants of King James I, and their name was changed to The King's Men. Shakespeare's final noncollaborative play, *The Famous History of the Life of Henry the Eighth,* was performed in London in 1613. Later that same year, he collaborated with John Fletcher to write a play called *The Two Noble Kinsmen.* At that time he was probably living again in Stratford, in a large house called New Place that he had bought in 1597. When he died in 1616, survived by his wife and his two daughters, Shakespeare was a wealthy man. He was buried in the Holy Trinity Church in Stratford-upon-Avon, where his bones rest to this day. The stone over his grave reads,

> Good frend for Jesus sake forbeare,
> To digg the dust encloased heare:
> Blest be the man that spares thes stones,
> And curst be he that moves my bones.

The Publication of Shakespeare's Plays

Shakespeare did not personally prepare his plays for publication, and no official collection of them appeared until after his death. A collection of his sonnets, considered by critics to be among the best ever written in English, appeared in 1609. Many individual plays were published during his lifetime in unauthorized editions known as quartos. Many of these quartos are quite unreliable. Some were probably based on actors' memories of the plays. Some were reprintings of so-called prompter's copies used in production of the plays. Some may have been based on final manuscript versions produced by the author. In 1623, seven years after Shakespeare's death, his friends and fellow actors John Heminge and Henry Condell published a collected edition of thirty-five of Shakespeare's plays. This collection is known to literary historians as the First Folio. In the centuries since 1623, and especially during the last century and a half, editors have worked diligently to compare the various early printed versions of Shakespeare's works to determine which version or versions of each play best represent Shakespeare's intent.

Shakespeare's Finest Achievement

Fragments can be tantalizing. They tempt people, awakening a desire to reconstruct the missing pieces. Since very little is known of Shakespeare's life beyond a few official records and comments in diaries or letters by others, many people have been driven to speculate about the private life of England's greatest author. Such speculation is made all the more difficult by the fact that Shakespeare did not write in a personal vein, about himself, but rather concentrated his vision on the lives of others. Reading his plays, or seeing them performed, we come to know many of his characters better than we know most people in our lives. A characteristic of Shakespeare's greatness is that his work takes us on journeys into parallel universes, into other minds, so that his characters' innermost feelings, dreams, wishes, values, motivations, and even contradictions become accessible. This is, perhaps, Shakespeare's finest achievement.

The Authorship of Shakespeare's Plays

The fact that Shakespeare was a commoner and led, according to the few facts we have, a rather ordinary life, has led many people to speculate that his plays were written by someone else—by the Earl of Oxford, perhaps, or by Ben Jonson, but there are good reasons to believe that Shakespeare was, indeed, the author of the plays attributed to him. One reason to accept the traditional attribution is that the plays show an understanding of the lives of people in all stations of life, from the lowliest peasants to men and women of the court. We know that Shakespeare came from a common background and later moved in court circles, and this fact is consistent with his understanding of people from all walks of life. At the very least, a careful reader must conclude that the plays attributed to Shakespeare are the work of a single author, for they have a distinct voice not to be found in the work of any other dramatist of his day—a voice that has enriched our language as none other has ever done.

The Uniqueness of Shakespeare's Work

No brief summary can begin to catalog the many virtues of Shakespeare's work. He was a gifted observer of people, capable of creating unforgettable characters from all stations and walks of life. He used one of the largest vocabularies ever employed by an author, filling his plays with concrete details and with speech that, while not always realistic, is always engaging and believable. His plays probe the range of human experience. They are romantic in the sense that they are filled with passions conveyed intensely. However, the plays rarely strain credibility or sink into sensationalism or sentimentality. Shakespeare's language tends to be dense, metaphorical, full of puns and word play, and yet natural, so that it comes "trippingly off the tongue" of an actor. A scene from Shakespeare tears across the stage, riveting and dramatic, and yet it bears close rereading, revealing in that rereading astonishing depth and complexity. Shakespeare used in his plays a combination of prose, rhymed poetry, and blank verse always appropriate to the character or scene at hand. His plays have given many, many phrases to the English language. They have filled audiences with laughter, joy, pity, fear, sadness, despair, and suspense for over four hundred years. In fact, his works have been performed more often and in more countries around the world than those of any other dramatist. To begin to read Shakespeare is to enter a world, one might say the world, for his art is, as Hamlet says it should be, "a mirror held up to nature"—to human nature. To read him well is to begin to understand others and ourselves. As Ben Jonson wrote, Shakespeare's art is "not of an age, but for all time."

Time Line of Shakespeare's Life

April 23, 1564	William Shakespeare is born in Stratford-upon-Avon to parents Mary Arden Shakespeare and John Shakespeare.
April 26, 1564	William Shakespeare is baptized.
1582	William Shakespeare marries Anne Hathaway.
1583	Shakespeare's first daughter, Susanna, is born and christened.
1585	Anne Hathaway Shakespeare gives birth to twins: a boy, Hamnet, and a girl, Judith.
1589–1591	Shakespeare's first histories, *Henry the Sixth,* Parts 1 and 2, are produced.
1592–1594	*The Tragedy of Richard the Third* is produced. Not long afterward, the plague afflicts London and the theaters close. Shakespeare writes *Venus and Adonis* and *The Rape of Lucrece.*
1592–1594	Shakespeare's first comedy, *The Comedy of Errors,* is produced.
c. 1593	Shakespeare begins his sonnet cycle.
1593–1594	*The Taming of the Shrew* is produced.
1594–1595	*Love's Labor's Lost* is produced.
1595	*The Tragedy of King Richard the Second* is produced.
1595–1596	*The Tragedy of Romeo and Juliet* and *A Midsummer Night's Dream* are produced.
1596–1597	*The Merchant of Venice* and *Henry the Fourth, Part 1* are produced.
1596	Shakespeare's son, Hamnet, dies at age eleven.
1597	Shakespeare acquires a fine home called New Place in Stratford-upon-Avon.
1597	Shakespeare produces *The Merry Wives of Windsor,* possibly at the request of Queen Elizabeth I.
1598	Shakespeare produces *Henry the Fourth, Part 2.*
1598–1599	*Much Ado about Nothing* is produced.
1599	*The Life of Henry the Fifth, The Tragedy of Julius Cæsar,* and *As You Like It* are produced.

Shakespeare's Globe Theater opens.

The Tragedy of Hamlet, Prince of Denmark is produced.

Twelfth Night, or What You Will and *The History of Troilus and Cressida* are produced.

All's Well That Ends Well is produced.

Queen Elizabeth I dies. Shakespeare's troupe serves James I and becomes known as the King's Men.

Measure for Measure and *The Tragedy of Othello, the Moor of Venice* are produced.

The Tragedy of King Lear is produced.

The Tragedy of Macbeth is produced.

The Tragedy of Antony and Cleopatra is produced.

The Tragedy of Coriolanus and *Pericles, Prince of Tyre* are produced.

Cymbeline is produced.

The Winter's Tale is produced.

The Tempest is produced.

The Famous History of the Life of Henry the Eighth is produced.

Shakespeare collaborates with John Fletcher to write *The Two Noble Kinsmen.*

Shakespeare dies and is buried in Holy Trinity Church in Stratford-upon-Avon.

Date
1599
1600–1601
1601–1602
1602–1603
1603
1604
1605
1606
1607
1607–1608
1609–1610
1610–1611
1611
1612–1613
1613
April 23, 1616

The Tempest

The Renaissance in England

The word *renaissance* means, literally, "rebirth." Historians use the word to refer to the period between the fifteenth and early seventeenth centuries when Europe was influenced by a rebirth of interest in Greek and Latin learning. This renewal of interest in classical learning and literature moved Europeans from medieval habits of thought toward more modern habits.

Rediscovering the arts and literature of classical Greece and Rome brought about, first in Italy and then in the rest of Europe, a renewed interest in human life on earth. The Renaissance devotion to Greek and Latin classics has thus become known as Humanism. Many Humanist philosophers believed that human beings were created in the image of God and that each person was a little world, or *microcosmos,* complete in himself or herself. They believed that humans, sharing as they did in the divine, could perfect themselves and the institutions of this world. Out of this belief came a new emphasis on learning and on the arts, as well as religious and political debates that led to the Protestant Reformation, the decline of feudalism, and the emergence of modern nationalism. Also, the invention of the printing press in 1453 allowed information to spread more quickly and encouraged people to read, to write, to think for themselves, and to challenge authority.

In England, the period from 1558 to 1603 is known as the Elizabethan Age after the queen who reigned during this period. English literature reached what many people consider to be its zenith during the Elizabethan Age. Shakespeare wrote and produced his plays at the height of the Elizabethan period and throughout much of the Jacobean period, the period from 1603 to 1625 when James I ruled England.

Shakespeare's writing is a good example of the spirit of the Renaissance—his plays often focus on memorable and complex characters, his plots often are derived from classical sources, and his themes often involve challenges to authority. Although Shakespeare's scholarly contemporary and fellow playwright Ben Jonson wrote of Shakespeare, "thou hadst small Latin, and less Greek," Shakespeare knew far more of these languages than most people do today, and he probably read many of the classical works of Rome in their original Latin. Play writing in Shakespeare's time was not so much a matter of inventing a subject and characters previously unknown to the stage as it was a process of adapting, alluding to, and drawing inspiration from both classical and contemporary sources. Shakespeare was inspired by classical works and by the history of Rome to write such plays as *The Tragedy of Julius Cæsar, The Tragedy of Antony and Cleopatra,* and *The Tragedy of Coriolanus.* While the plots of these plays are derived from classical sources, Shakespeare also was inspired by and reworked the stories and plays of his contemporaries to produce *The Tragedy of Romeo and Juliet, As You Like It,* and other plays. Shakespeare also developed his own plots for which no source is known in plays such as *A Midsummer Night's Dream* and *The Tempest.* Even these works, however, are filled with classical and contemporary allusions.

Types of Renaissance Drama

The two most common types of drama during the English Renaissance were comedies and tragedies. The key difference between comedies and tragedies is that the former have happy endings and the latter have unhappy ones. It is only a slight exaggeration to say that Renaissance comedies end with wedding bells and tragedies with funeral bells.

A **comedy** is typically lighthearted, though it may contain serious action and themes. Action in a comedy usually progresses from initial order to a humorous misunderstanding or confusion and back to order again. Stock elements of comedy include mistaken identities, puns and word play, and coarse or exaggerated characters. Shakespeare's comedies frequently lead to one or more marriages.

A **tragedy** tells the story of the downfall of a person of high status. Often it celebrates the courage and dignity of its hero in the face of inevitable doom. The hero is typically neither completely good nor completely evil but somewhere between these extremes. The hero's fall may be brought about by some flaw in his or her character, known as a **tragic flaw.**

Another kind of popular play produced during this period was the **history**, or play about events from the past. Shakespeare frequently used elements of tragedy in his histories, although some of his histories also used comic elements. In Renaissance England, **masques** were also popular. These were elaborate shows that featured acting, music, and dance. The actors were often lavishly costumed and masked. Masques were popular in both the court of Elizabeth I and the court of James I, and their theme was often an allegorical or mythological compliment to the noble or group of nobles for whom they were performed. Shakespeare often included elements of masques in his plays, such as processions or masked dances.

Four of Shakespeare's late plays—*Pericles, Prince of Tyre; Cymbeline; The Winter's Tale;* and *The Tempest*—that were originally classified as comedies have been reclassified as romances by later scholars. **Romances** are theatrical and nonrealistic. They frequently employ fantastic elements such as fairies and magical spells. They combine comic and tragic themes, and contain plots that move towards reunion, reconciliation, and regeneration. Standard devices in romances include music and song; the changing of old garments for fresh ones to signify transformation; and startling spectacles, or surprising and visually striking scenes—such as the reunion of characters who have believed each other to be dead—that make the audience question the relationship between reality and illusion.

The Political Conditions of Theater in Renaissance London

In the late sixteenth century, London was a bustling city of perhaps 150,000 people—the mercantile, political, and artistic center of England. The city proper was ruled by a mayor and aldermen who frowned upon theater because it brought together large crowds of people, creating the potential for lawlessness and the spread of controversial ideas and disease. Many times during the period, London city officials or Parliament ordered the theaters closed, once because they objected to the political content of a play called *Isle of Dogs,* and regularly because of outbreaks of plague. Parliament, which was dominated by Puritans, passed laws that made it possible for traveling actors and other performers to be arrested as vagabonds and cruelly punished. For protection, actors sought the patronage of members of the nobility. Actors would become, technically, servants of a famous lord and go by such names as The Lord Worcester's Men.

Fortunately for actors and playwrights, Queen Elizabeth and other members of the nobility loved the theater and protected it. Elizabeth herself maintained two troupes of boy actors, connected to her royal chapels. In addition to these acting troupes made up of boys, London boasted several professional troupes made up of men. In those days, women did not act, and women's roles were played by men, a fact that further increased Puritan disapproval of the theaters. When the Puritans took control of England in 1642, theater was banned altogether.

The Renaissance Playhouse

In 1576, James Burbage built the first professional playhouse in England. Burbage located his playhouse, which he called simply "the Theater," just outside the northern boundaries of the City of London, where he could avoid control by city authorities. Another professional theater, the Curtain, was built nearby shortly thereafter. In 1598, Burbage and other members of his theater company, the Lord Chamberlain's Men, tore down the Theater and used its materials to build a new playhouse, the Globe Theater, south of the city on the banks of the river Thames. One of the shareholders in the Globe was William Shakespeare.

From contemporary drawings and descriptions and from evidence in plays, we can reconstruct what Shakespeare's Globe must have looked like. The building was octagonal, or eight-sided, its walls covered by peaked, thatched roofs (see illustration, next page). The center of this "wooden O," as Shakespeare called it, was open to the air. The stage projected into the middle of this open space, and poorer theatergoers called "groundlings," who paid a penny apiece for admission, stood around three sides of the stage. Wealthier theatergoers could pay an additional penny or two and sit in one of the three tiers, or stories, of seats in the walls of the theater. In many respects, the theater was similar to medieval stages—a wagon pulled into the open courtyard of an inn, with the inn's balconies around it.

The stage itself was partially covered by a canopy supported by two large pillars. Trapdoors in the stage floor allowed for appearances by spirits or fairies and for the disappearance of bodies. Behind the stage, between the pillars, was an inner area called the "tiring house" that could be used for changing costumes and for indoor scenes such as throne rooms, bedchambers, and taverns. On either side of the stage were doors for entrances and exits. At the back of the tiring house was a

door and stairway that led to a second-level playing area that could be used as a hilltop, a castle turret, or a balcony (perhaps for the famous balcony scene from *Romeo and Juliet*). On the third level, above this balcony area, was an area for musicians and sound-effects people. A cannon shot from this area during a performance of Shakespeare's *Henry the Eighth* in 1613 caused a fire that burned the Globe to the ground.

Because the playhouse was open to the air, plays were presented in the daytime, and there was little or no artificial lighting. Scenery in the modern sense was nonexistent, and very few properties were used, beyond an occasional table or chair. Audiences had to use their imaginations to create the scenes, and playwrights helped their audiences to do this by writing descriptions of scenes into their characters' speeches.

The Renaissance Audience

Audiences at the Globe and similar theaters were quite mixed, or heterogeneous. They included people from all stations of society: laboring people from the lower classes, middle-class merchants, members of Parliament, and lords and ladies. Pickpockets mingled among the noisy, raucous groundlings crowded around the stage. Noble men and women sat on cushioned seats in the first-tier balcony. The fanfare of trumpets that signaled the beginning of a play was heard by some twenty-five hundred people, a cross section of the Elizabethan world. That Shakespeare's plays have such universal appeal may be explained by this fact: they were written for everyone, from "the most able, to him that can but spell."

The Tempest in Context

The Tempest is a romance that deals with magic, love and marriage, plots to gain or regain political power, the discovery of new lands, and the relationship between nature and civilization or art. A writer's themes are inevitably linked to the time in which he or she lives. The Renaissance was a time of political conflict and controversy both in England and in Europe as a whole. The Protestant Reformation sparked debate and open conflict between Catholics and Protestants; Henry VIII, founder of the Tudor Dynasty that ended with Elizabeth I's death, broke England away from the Church of Rome; Queen Mary I, known as "Bloody Mary," led the Counter-Reformation in England; rivalry between Spain and England led to the defeat of the Spanish Armada in 1588—these were only a few of the political clashes that shaped Shakespeare's view of the world. The main conflict in *The Tempest* is political—a duke named Prospero seeks redress upon his brother and a king who have conspired to rob him of his throne. In Shakespeare's time, political conflicts were often resolved through marriage; Prospero's scheme to marry his daughter to the son of the king who conspired against him reflects this Renaissance custom of political resolution achieved by marriage.

The Renaissance was not only a time of conflict but an era of discovery. In 1492, Christopher Columbus reached the Bahamas in the Americas, opening up a "New World" of wealth and resources for Spanish exploitation. After Columbus's initial voyage, European powers competed with one another to seize the opportunity that they imagined the "New World" offered them. In the process, Europeans devastated native populations across the Americas. By the time Shakespeare wrote *The Tempest,* two colonies had been founded in North America, one the unsuccessful Roanoke colony founded by Sir Walter Raleigh in 1587 and the other the Jamestown colony which was founded in 1607 and was still struggling to survive by 1611. In 1609, a small fleet of ships was sailing to Jamestown, and one was lost. Its crew was presumed dead, but in fact they did eventually arrive in Jamestown, after having run aground on the previously unexplored island of Bermuda. The news of this new island and the shipwreck and survival of the crew excited attention in England. Pamphlets about this discovery and other similar pamphlets about shipwrecks, sea-adventures, and exploration became a popular form of literature in England. Shakespeare used some of these pamphlets about Bermuda as sources when writing *The Tempest,* which is set on a remote island that resembles both this island of the "New World" and a Mediterranean island.

The contact with the natives of the New World inspired extreme responses among Europeans. Some colonists and explorers, motivated by greed and ambition, enslaved native peoples and exploited them. Sometimes, native peoples were brought back to England and displayed to curious crowds. A few Europeans reacted much differently to encounters with people from the new world. For example, French essayist Michel de Montaigne learned about the culture of the natives of Brazil and wrote a famous essay, "Of Cannibals," which praises the "natural" society of the natives and condemns the sometimes more brutal "civilized" society of Europeans. Shakespeare used Montaigne's essay as a source, forming his own individual response to Montaigne's ideas about a "natural" society.

The Tempest is one of Shakespeare's final plays and his last romance; it is followed only by *The Famous History of the Life of Henry the Eighth* and *The Two Noble Kinsmen.* Much has been made of *The Tempest* as Shakespeare's goodbye to the theater and his art. While this is certainly one possible view of *The Tempest,* it should be remembered that Shakespeare was only forty-seven when it was produced, he did write two more plays, and he probably intended to write several more. As one of his final plays and as a romance, *The Tempest* displays Shakespeare's genius for both tragedy and comedy. Serious themes and scenes are developed alongside more lighthearted, comic ones. Like most of Shakespeare's romances, *The Tempest* moves toward achieving reconciliation and regeneration, but many serious issues remain unresolved. These unresolved issues only add to the complexity of a play that is filled with fantastic spectacles and characters, a play that contains more music and song than any other of Shakespeare's works.

Echoes

Jaques.   All the world's a stage,
And all the men and women merely players;
They have their exits and their entrances,
And one man in his time plays many parts.

—As You Like It

Theseus.   The Poet's eye, in a fine frenzy rolling,
Doth glance from heaven to earth,
from earth to heaven;
And as imagination bodies forth
The forms of things unknown, the poet's pen
Turns them to shapes, and gives to aery nothing
A local habitation and a name.

—A Midsummer Night's Dream

Prologue.
O for a Muse of fire, that would ascend
The brightest heaven of invention!
A kingdom for a stage, princes to act,
And monarchs to behold the swelling scene!
Then should the warlike Harry, like himself,
Assume the port of Mars, and at his heels
(Leash'd in, like hounds) should famine, sword, and fire
Crouch for employment. But pardon, gentles all,
The flat unraised spirits that hath dar'd
On this unworthy scaffold to bring forth
So great an object. Can this cockpit hold
The vasty fields of France? Or may we cram
Within this wooden O the very casques
That did affright the air at Agincourt?
O, pardon! since a crooked figure may
Attest in little place a million,
And let us, ciphers to this great accompt,
On your imaginary forces work.

—The Life of Henry the Fifth

Dramatis Personae

ALONSO, *King of Naples*

SEBASTIAN, *his brother*

PROSPERO, *the rightful Duke of Milan*

ANTONIO, *his brother, the usurping Duke of Milan*

FERDINAND, *son to the King of Naples*

GONZALO, *an honest old councillor*

ADRIAN, *and* FRANCISCO, *lords*

CALIBAN, *a savage and deformed slave*

TRINCULO, *a jester*

STEPHANO, *a drunken butler*

MASTER OF A SHIP

BOATSWAIN

MARINERS

MIRANDA, *daughter to Prospero*

ARIEL, *an airy Spirit*

IRIS,

CERES,

JUNO,   *spirits*

NYMPHS,

REAPERS,

Other SPIRITS *attending on Prospero*

THE SCENE: A ship at sea; an uninhabited island.

Act I

**SCENE i: On a ship at sea: a tempestuous noise of thunder
and lightning heard.**

Enter a SHIP-MASTER *and a* BOATSWAIN.[1]

MASTER.   Boatswain!

BOATSWAIN.   Here, master: what cheer?

MASTER.   Good; speak to th' mariners: Fall to't,[2] yarely,[3]
or we run ourselves aground. Bestir,[4] bestir.   *Exit.*

Enter MARINERS.

5   BOATSWAIN.   Heigh, my hearts! cheerly, cheerly, my
hearts! yare, yare! Take in the topsail. Tend to th'
master's whistle.—Blow,[5] till thou burst thy wind, if
room[6] enough!

Enter ALONSO, SEBASTIAN, ANTONIO, FERDINAND, GONZALO,
and OTHERS.

ALONSO.   Good boatswain, have care. Where's the
10   master? Play[7] the men.

BOATSWAIN.   I pray now keep below.

ANTONIO.   Where is the master, bos'n?

BOATSWAIN.   Do you not hear him? You mar our labor.
Keep your cabins; you do assist the storm.

15   GONZALO.   Nay, good, be patient.

BOATSWAIN. When the sea is. Hence! What cares these
roarers[8] for the name of king? To cabin! silence! trouble
us not.

GONZALO.   Good, yet remember whom thou hast aboard.

20   BOATSWAIN.   None that I more love than myself. You
are a councillor; if you can command these elements to
silence, and work the peace of the present, we will not
hand a rope more. Use your authority. If you cannot,

Side notes:

◄ *Where is this scene set? What danger are the characters facing?*

◄ *What does the boatswain want the noblemen to do? Why is he rude? What does he point out about the limits of kingly power?*

ACT I, SCENE i

1. **Boatswain.** Petty officer in charge of the deck crew on a ship
2. **to't.** To it
3. **yarely.** Smartly, quickly
4. **Bestir.** Stir into action
5. **Blow.** He is addressing the storm
6. **room.** Space to maneuver the boat
7. **Play.** Ply, or urge to work
8. **roarers.** Loud, turbulent waves

▶ What comforts
Gonzalo?

25 give thanks you have liv'd so long, and make yourself
ready in your cabin for the mischance of the hour, if it
so hap.[9]—Cheerly, good hearts! Out of our way, I say.

Exit.

GONZALO.   I have great comfort from this fellow.
Methinks he hath no drowning mark upon him, his
complexion is perfect gallows.[10] Stand fast, good Fate,
30 to his hanging, make the rope of his destiny our cable,[11]
for our own doth little advantage. If he be not born to
be hang'd, our case is miserable.

Exeunt.

Enter BOATSWAIN.

BOATSWAIN.   Down with the topmast! Yare! lower,
lower! bring her to try with main-course. [*A cry within.*]
35 A plague upon this howling! they are louder than the
weather, or our office.

Enter SEBASTIAN, ANTONIO, *and* GONZALO.

Yet again? What do you here? Shall we give o'er and
drown? Have you a mind to sink?

SEBASTIAN.   A pox o' your throat, you bawling,
40 blasphemous, incharitable dog!

BOATSWAIN.   Work you then.

ANTONIO.   Hang, cur![12] hang, you whoreson, insolent
noisemaker! We are less afraid to be drown'd than thou
art.

45 GONZALO.   I'll warrant him for drowning, though the
ship were no stronger than a nutshell, and as leaky as an
unstanch'd wench.

BOATSWAIN.   Lay her a-hold, a-hold! Set her two courses
off to sea again! Lay her off.

Enter MARINERS *wet.*

50 MARINERS.   All lost! To prayers, to prayers! All lost!

Exeunt.

BOATSWAIN.   What, must our mouths be cold?

GONZALO.   The King and Prince at prayers, let's assist
them,
For our case is as theirs.

---

9. **hap.** Happens
10. **Methinks . . . gallows.** Referring to the old proverb "He that is born to be
hanged will never be drowned"
11. **make the rope . . . our cable.** May the rope that will hang him anchor our
ship.
12. **cur.** Dog

SEBASTIAN.   I am out of patience.

ANTONIO.   We are merely cheated of our lives by
    drunkards.
55 This wide-chopp'd rascal—would thou mightst lie
    drowning.
    The washing of ten tides!

GONZALO.   He'll be hang'd yet,
    Though every drop of water swear against it,
    And gape at wid'st to glut[13] him.
              [*A confused noise within.*] "Mercy on us!"—
    "We split, we split!"—"Farewell, my wife and children!"—
60 "Farewell, brother!"—"We split, we split, we split!"
                                          Exit BOATSWAIN.

ANTONIO.   Let's all sink wi' th' King.

SEBASTIAN.   Let's take leave of him.   *Exit with* ANTONIO.

GONZALO.   Now would I give a thousand furlongs[14] of
    sea for an acre of barren ground, long heath, brown
65 furze,[15] any thing. The wills above be done! but I would
    fain[16] die a dry death.   *Exit.*

◄ What is happening to the ship? What do Antonio and Sebastian expect will happen to them? What does Gonzalo long for?

SCENE **ii: An island. Before Prospero's cell.**

Enter PROSPERO *and* MIRANDA.

MIRANDA.   If by your art,[1] my dearest father, you have
    Put the wild waters in this roar, <u>allay</u> them.
    The sky it seems would pour down stinking pitch,
    But that the sea, mounting to th' welkin's[2] cheek,
5   Dashes the fire out. O! I have suffered
    With those that I saw suffer. A brave vessel
    (Who had, no doubt, some noble creature in her)
    Dash'd all to pieces! O, the cry did knock
    Against my very heart. Poor souls, they perish'd.

◄ What does Miranda ask her father to do? What does she think caused the tempest? What has made Miranda suffer?

---

13. **glut.** Swallow
14. **furlong.** Unit of measure equal to one eighth of a mile
15. **furze.** Prickly evergreen shrub
16. **fain.** Rather, gladly

ACT I, SCENE ii

1. **art.** Magic
2. **welkin's.** Sky's

**Words
For
Everyday
Use**   **al • lay** (a lā´) *vt.,* calm

10   Had I been any God of power, I would
      Have sunk the sea within the earth or ere
      It should the good ship so have swallow'd, and
      The fraughting[3] souls within her.

PROSPERO.   Be collected:
      No more amazement. Tell your piteous[4] heart
15   There's no harm done.

MIRANDA.   O woe the day!

▶ Of what does Prospero say Miranda is ignorant?

PROSPERO.   No harm:
      I have done nothing, but in care of thee
      (Of thee my dear one, thee my daughter), who
      Art ignorant of what thou art, nought knowing
      Of whence I am, nor that I am more better
20   Than Prospero, master of a full poor <u>cell</u>,
      And thy no greater father.

MIRANDA.   More to know
      Did never meddle with my thoughts.

PROSPERO.   'Tis time
      I should inform thee farther. Lend thy hand,
      And pluck my magic garment from me. So,
                        Lays down his mantle.

▶ What does Prospero reveal about the ship and the storm?

25   Lie there, my art. Wipe thou thine eyes, have comfort.
      The direful spectacle of the wrack, which touch'd
      The very virtue of compassion in thee,
      I have with such provision in mine art
      So safely ordered that there is no soul—
30   No, not so much <u>perdition</u> as an hair
      Betid[5] to any creature in the vessel
      Which thou heard'st cry, which thou saw'st sink. Sit
           down,
      For thou must now know farther.

MIRANDA.   You have often
      Begun to tell me what I am, but stopp'd
35   And left me to a bootless inquisition,[6]
      Concluding "Stay: not yet."

---

3. **fraughting.** Filling
4. **piteous.** Full of pity
5. **Betid.** Happened
6. **bootless inquisition.** Useless inquiry

Words For Everyday Use

cell (sel) *n.*, small room or cubicle
per • di • tion (pər dish´ən) *n.*, loss, ruin

PROSPERO. The hour's now come.
The very minute bids thee ope thine ear.
Obey,[7] and be attentive. Canst thou remember
A time before we came unto this cell?
40 I do not think thou canst, for then thou wast not
Out three years old.

MIRANDA. Certainly, sir, I can.

PROSPERO. By what? by any other house, or person?
Of any thing the image, tell me, that
Hath kept with thy remembrance.

MIRANDA. 'Tis far off;
45 And rather like a dream than an assurance
That my remembrance warrants. Had I not
Four, or five, women once that tended me?

PROSPERO. Thou hadst; and more, Miranda. But how is
it
That this lives in thy mind? What seest thou else
50 In the dark backward and <u>abysm</u> of time?
If thou remember'st aught ere thou cam'st here,
How thou cam'st here thou mayst.

MIRANDA. But that I do not.

PROSPERO. Twelve year since,[8] Miranda, twelve year
since,
Thy father was the Duke of Milan and
55 A prince of power.

◄ *What position did Prospero once hold?*

MIRANDA. Sir, are not you my father?

PROSPERO. Thy mother was a piece[9] of virtue, and
She said thou wast my daughter; and thy father
Was Duke of Milan, and his only heir
And princess no worse issued.[10]

MIRANDA. O the heavens,
60 What foul play had we, that we came from thence?
Or blessed was't we did?

PROSPERO. Both, both, my girl.

---

7. **Obey.** Listen
8. **Twelve year since.** Twelve years ago
9. **piece.** Masterpiece
10. **no worse issued.** No less noble by blood

Words For Everyday Use a • **bysm** (ə biz´əm) *n.*, abyss

By foul play (as thou say'st) were we heav'd thence,
But blessedly holp[11] hither.

MIRANDA.   O, my heart bleeds
To think o' th' teen[12] that I have turn'd you to,
65 Which is from my remembrance! Please you, farther.

PROSPERO.   My brother and thy uncle, call'd Antonio—
I pray thee mark me—that a brother should
Be so <u>perfidious</u>!—he whom next thyself
Of all the world I lov'd, and to him put
70 The manage of my state, as at that time
Through all the signories[13] it was the first,
And Prospero the prime duke, being so reputed
In dignity, and for the liberal arts
Without a parallel; those being all my study,
75 The government I cast upon my brother,
And to my state grew stranger, being transported
And rapt[14] in secret studies. Thy false uncle—
Dost thou attend me?

MIRANDA.   Sir, most heedfully.

PROSPERO.   Being once perfected how to grant suits,
80 How to deny them, who t' advance and who
To trash for overtopping,[15] new created
The creatures that were mine, I say, or chang'd 'em,
Or else new form'd 'em; having both the key
Of officer and office, set all hearts i' th' state
85 To what tune pleas'd his ear, that now he was
The ivy which had hid my princely trunk,
And suck'd my verdure[16] out on't. Thou attend'st not!

MIRANDA.   O, good sir, I do.

PROSPERO.   I pray thee mark me.
I, thus neglecting worldly ends, all dedicated
90 To closeness and the bettering of my mind
With that which, but by being so retir'd,

► Who was responsible for the "foul play" that bereaved Prospero of his dukedom? What authority did Prospero give Antonio? Why did he give him this authority?

► Does Prospero accept any responsibility for what happened to his dukedom? Why, or why not?

---

11. **holp.** Helped
12. **teen.** Sadness, trouble
13. **signories.** Cities
14. **rapt.** Completely absorbed in
15. **trash for over-topping.** Keep from becoming overly powerful
16. **verdure.** Vigor; energy

Words For Everyday Use	**per • fid • i • ous** (pər fid´ē əs) *adj.*, treacherous; faithless

O'er-priz'd all popular rate, in my false brother
Awak'd an evil nature, and my trust,
Like a good parent, did beget[17] of him
95 A falsehood in its contrary, as great
As my trust was, which had indeed no limit,
A confidence sans[18] bound. He being thus lorded,
Not only with what my revenue yielded,
But what my power might else exact—like one
100 Who having into truth, by telling of it,
Made such a sinner of his memory
To credit his own lie—he did believe
He was indeed the Duke, out o' th' substitution,
And executing th' outward face of royalty
105 With all <u>prerogative</u>. Hence his ambition growing—
Dost thou hear?

MIRANDA.   Your tale, sir, would cure deafness.

PROSPERO.   To have no screen between this part he
    play'd
And him he play'd it for, he needs will be
Absolute Milan[19]—me (poor man) my library
110 Was dukedom large enough: of temporal royalties[20]
He thinks me now incapable; confederates[21]
(So dry he was for sway)[22] wi' th' King of Naples
To give him annual tribute, do him homage,
Subject his coronet to his crown, and bend
115 The dukedom yet unbow'd (alas, poor Milan!)
To most ignoble stooping.

MIRANDA.   O the heavens!

PROSPERO.   Mark his condition, and th' event, then tell
    me
If this might be a brother.

MIRANDA.   I should sin
To think but nobly of my grandmother.
120 Good wombs have borne bad sons.

---

17. **beget.** Bring into being
18. **sans.** Without
19. **Absolute Milan.** Actual duke of Milan
20. **temporal royalties.** Royal duties
21. **confederates.** Conspires or makes alliance with
22. **dry . . . sway.** Eager for peace

◄ How many times has Prospero accused Miranda of not listening? Does Miranda seem to be listening? What does this reveal about how Prospero feels when speaking of his lost dukedom?

◄ With whom did Antonio align himself to gain the dukedom? What did he promise this person?

Words For Everyday Use
pre • rog • a • tive (prē răg´ə tiv) *n.,* right or privilege

PROSPERO. Now the condition.
The King of Naples, being an enemy
To me <u>inveterate</u>, hearkens my brother's suit,
Which was, that he, in lieu o'[23] the premises
Of homage, and I know not how much tribute,
125 Should presently <u>extirpate</u> me and mine
Out of the dukedom, and confer fair Milan
With all the honors on my brother; whereon,
A treacherous army levied, one midnight
Fated to th' purpose, did Antonio open
130 The gates of Milan, and, i' th' dead of darkness
The ministers for th' purpose hurried thence
Me and thy crying self.

MIRANDA. Alack, for pity!
I, not remembering how I cried out then,
Will cry it o'er again. It is a hint
135 That wrings mine eyes to't.

PROSPERO. Hear a little further,
And then I'll bring thee to the present business
Which now's upon 's; without the which this story
Were most impertinent.[24]

MIRANDA. Wherefore did they not
That hour destroy us?

PROSPERO. Well demanded, wench;
140 My tale provokes that question. Dear, they durst[25] not,
So dear the love my people bore me; nor set
A mark so bloody on the business; but
With colors fairer painted their foul ends.
In few, they hurried us aboard a bark,[26]
145 Bore us some leagues to sea; where they prepared
A rotten carcass of a butt, not rigg'd,
Nor tackle, sail, nor mast, the very rats
Instinctively have quit it. There they hoist us,
To cry to th' sea, that roar'd to us; to sigh
150 To th' winds whose pity, sighing back again,
Did us but loving wrong.

► *Whose army marched into Milan? Who let the army into the city?*

► *Why didn't the traitors kill Prospero and Miranda? What did they do to them?*

---

23. **in lieu o'**. In exchange for
24. **impertinent**. Irrelevant
25. **durst**. Dared
26. **bark**. Ship

Words For Everyday Use

in • vet • er • ate (in vet´ər it) *adj.*, firmly established
ex • tir • pate (ek´stər pāt´) *vt.*, destroy

MIRANDA.   Alack, what trouble
Was I then to you!

PROSPERO.   O, a cherubin[27]
Thou wast that did preserve me. Thou didst smile,
Infused with a fortitude from heaven,
155 When I have deck'd the sea with drops full salt,
Under my burthen[28] groan'd, which rais'd in me
An undergoing stomach, to bear up
Against what should ensue.

MIRANDA.   How came we ashore?

PROSPERO.   By Providence divine.
160 Some food we had, and some fresh water, that
A noble Neapolitan, Gonzalo,
Out of his charity, who being then appointed
Master of this design, did give us, with
Rich garments, linens, stuffs, and necessaries,
165 Which since have steaded much;[29] so, of his gentleness,
Knowing I lov'd my books, he furnish'd me
From mine own library with volumes[30] that
I prize above my dukedom.

MIRANDA.   Would I might
But ever see that man!

PROSPERO.   Now I arise.   *Puts on his robe.*
170 Sit still, and hear the last of our sea-sorrow:
Here in this island we arriv'd; and here
Have I, thy schoolmaster, made thee more profit
Than other princess' can, that have more time
For vainer hours, and tutors not so careful.

175 MIRANDA.   Heavens thank you for't! And now, I pray
        you, sir,
For still 'tis beating in my mind, your reason
For raising this sea-storm?

PROSPERO.   Know thus far forth:
By accident most strange, bountiful Fortune

◀ Who helped
Miranda and
Prospero survive to
reach shore? What
did this person give
them? What does
this information
reveal about this
character?

◀ What reason
does Prospero give
Miranda for raising
the storm?

---

27. **cherubin.** Angel; sweet, innocent child
28. **burthen.** Burden
29. **steaded much.** Been very useful
30. **volumes.** Prospero's books of magic

Words
For
Everyday
Use

en • sue (en sōō´) *vi.,* come afterward; follow immediately

(Now my dear lady) hath mine enemies
180 Brought to this shore; and by my <u>prescience</u>
I find my zenith[31] doth depend upon
A most <u>auspicious</u> star, whose influence
If now I court not, but omit,[32] my fortunes
Will ever after droop. Here cease more questions.
185 Thou art inclin'd to sleep; 'tis a good dullness,
And give it way. I know thou canst not choose.

MIRANDA *sleeps.*

Come away, servant, come; I am ready now,
Approach, my Ariel. Come.

Enter ARIEL.

ARIEL.   All hail, great master, grave sir, hail! I come
190 To answer thy best pleasure; be't to fly,
To swim, to dive into the fire, to ride
On the curl'd clouds. To thy strong bidding, task
Ariel, and all his quality.

PROSPERO.   Hast thou, spirit,
Perform'd to point the tempest that I bade thee?

195 ARIEL.   To every article.
I boarded the King's ship; now on the beak,
Now in the waist, the deck, in every cabin,
I flam'd amazement:[33] Sometime I'ld divide,
And burn in many places; on the topmast,
200 The yards and boresprit, would I flame distinctly,
Then meet and join. Jove's[34] lightning, the precursors
O' th' dreadful thunder-claps, more momentary
And sight-outrunning were not; the fire and cracks
Of sulphurous roaring the most mighty Neptune[35]
205 Seem to besiege, and make his bold waves tremble,
Yea, his dread trident shake.

PROSPERO.   My brave spirit!
Who was so firm, so constant, that this coil[36]

▶ *What caused the tempest?*

---

31. **zenith.** Height of fortune
32. **omit.** Fail to take advantage of
33. **flam'd amazement.** Struck terror by appearing as flames also called St. Elmo's Fire
34. **Jove's.** Jove was the Roman god of the heavens and of lightning.
35. **Neptune.** Roman god of the sea who caused earthquakes with his trident
36. **coil.** Uproar

Words For Everyday Use	**pres • ci • ence** (presh´əns) *n.,* foreknowledge **aus • pi • cious** (ôs pish´ əs) *adj.,* favorable

Would not infect his reason?

ARIEL.   Not a soul
But felt a fever of the mad,[37] and play'd
210 Some tricks of desperation. All but mariners
Plung'd in the foaming brine, and quit the vessel.
Then all afire with me, the King's son, Ferdinand,
With hair up-staring (then like reeds, not hair),
Was the first man that leapt; cried, "Hell is empty,
215 And all the devils are here."

PROSPERO.   Why, that's my spirit!
But was not this nigh shore?

ARIEL.   Close by, my master.

PROSPERO.   But are they, Ariel, safe?

ARIEL.   Not a hair perish'd;
On their sustaining garments not a blemish,
But fresher than before; and as thou badst[38] me,
220 In troops I have dispers'd them 'bout the isle.
The King's son have I landed by himself,
Whom I left cooling of the air with sighs,
In an odd angle of the isle, and sitting,
His arms in this sad knot.[39]

PROSPERO.   Of the King's ship,
225 The mariners, say how thou hast dispos'd,
And all the rest o' th' fleet.

ARIEL.   Safely in harbor
Is the King's ship; in the deep nook, where once
Thou call'dst me up at midnight to fetch dew
From the still-vex'd Bermoothes,[40] there she's hid;
230 The mariners all under hatches stowed;
Who, with a charm join'd to their suff'red labor,
I have left asleep; and for the rest o' th' fleet
(Which I dispers'd), they all have met again,
And are upon the Mediterranean float[41]
235 Bound sadly home for Naples,
Supposing that they saw the King's ship wrack'd,
And his great person perish.

PROSPERO.   Ariel, thy charge
Exactly is perform'd; but there's more work.
What is the time o' th' day?

◄ *What happened aboard the ship?*

◄ *What happened to the people who jumped off the ship?*

◄ *Whom did Ariel leave in "an odd angle of the isle"?*

◄ *What has happened to the mariners aboard the king's ship? What do the people aboard the rest of the king's fleet of vessels believe?*

---

37. **felt . . . mad.** Felt as madmen feel
38. **badst.** Bade, urged
39. **arms . . . sad knot.** Arms crossed sadly
40. **Bermoothes.** Islands of Bermuda, known for their storms
41. **float.** Flood, sea

ARIEL.   Past the mid season.

240 **PROSPERO.**   At least two glasses.[42] The time 'twixt six
and now
Must by us both be spent most preciously.

► *What does Ariel want from Prospero? Why does Ariel believe that he deserves this? Why won't Prospero do this for Ariel?*

ARIEL.   Is there more toil? Since thou dost give me pains,
Let me remember thee what thou hast promis'd,
Which is not yet perform'd me.

PROSPERO.   How now? moody?
245 What is't thou canst demand?

ARIEL.   My liberty.

PROSPERO.   Before the time be out? No more!

ARIEL.   I prithee,[43]
Remember I have done thee worthy service,
Told thee no lies, made thee no mistakings, serv'd
Without or grudge or grumblings. Thou did promise
250 To bate[44] me a full year.

PROSPERO.   Dost thou forget
From what a torment I did free thee?

ARIEL.   No.

PROSPERO.   Thou dost; and think'st it much to tread the
ooze
Of the salt deep,
To run upon the sharp wind of the north,
255 To do me business in the veins o' th' earth
When it is bak'd with frost.

ARIEL.   I do not, sir.

PROSPERO.   Thou liest, <u>malignant</u> thing! Hast thou
forgot
The foul witch Sycorax, who with age and envy
Was grown into a hoop? Hast thou forgot her?

260 **ARIEL.**   No, sir.

PROSPERO.   Thou hast. Where was she born? Speak.
Tell me.

ARIEL.   Sir, in Argier.[45]

---

42. **two glasses.** Two o'clock
43. **prithee.** Pray thee, beg thee
44. **bate.** Abate, lessen the span of Ariel's service
45. **Argier.** Algiers, capital of Algeria

Words For Everyday Use	**ma • lig • nant** (mə ligʹnənt) *adj.*, having evil influence; harmful

PROSPERO.   O, was she so? I must
Once in a month recount what thou hast been,
Which thou forget'st. This damn'd witch Sycorax,
For mischiefs manifold, and sorceries terrible
265   To enter human hearing, from Argier,
Thou know'st was banish'd; for one thing she did
They would not take her life. Is not this true?

ARIEL.   Ay, sir.

PROSPERO.   This blue-eyed hag was hither brought with
        child
270   And here was left by th' sailors. Thou, my slave,
As thou report'st thyself, was then her servant,
And for thou wast a spirit too delicate
To act her earthy and abhorr'd commands,
Refusing her grand hests,[46] she did confine thee,
275   By help of her more potent ministers,
And in her most <u>unmitigable</u> rage,
Into a cloven pine, within which rift
Imprison'd, thou didst painfully remain
A dozen years; within which space she died,
280   And left thee there, where thou didst vent thy groans
As fast as mill-wheels strike. Then was this island
(Save for the son that she did litter here,
A freckled whelp[47] hag-born) not honor'd with
A human shape.

ARIEL.   Yes—Caliban her son.

285   PROSPERO.   Dull thing, I say so; he, that Caliban
Whom now I keep in service. Thou best know'st
What torment I did find thee in; thy groans
Did make wolves howl and penetrate the breasts
Of ever-angry bears. It was a torment
290   To lay upon the damn'd, which Sycorax
Could not again undo. It was mine art,
When I arriv'd and heard thee, that made gape
The pine, and let thee out.

ARIEL.   I thank thee, master.

PROSPERO.   If thou more murmur'st, I will rend an oak

◄ Who used to live on the island? Whom did this person bring with her?

◄ What did Sycorax do to Ariel? Why?

◄ Who else serves Prospero? How does Prospero seem to feel about this person?

◄ Why must Ariel serve Prospero?

46. **hests.** Commands
47. **whelp.** Term of contempt for a child

Words For Everyday Use
un • mit • i • ga • ble (un mit´ə gə´bəl) *adj.*, absolute; unstoppable

► What does
Prospero promise to
do?

295 And peg thee in his knotty entrails till
Thou hast howl'd away twelve winters.

ARIEL.   Pardon, master;
I will be correspondent to command
And do my spriting gently.

PROSPERO.   Do so; and after two days
I will discharge thee.

ARIEL.   That's my noble master!
300 What shall I do? Say what? what shall I do?

PROSPERO.   Go make thyself like a nymph o' th' sea; be
    subject
To no sight but thine and mine, invisible
To every eyeball else. Go take this shape
And hither come in't. Go. Hence with diligence!

                                        Exit ARIEL.

305 Awake, dear heart, awake! Thou hast slept well,
Awake!

MIRANDA.   The strangeness of your story put
Heaviness in me.

PROSPERO.   Shake it off. Come on,
We'll visit Caliban my slave, who never
Yields us kind answer.

►How does Miranda
feel about Caliban?
Why do Miranda and
Prospero need
Caliban?

MIRANDA.   'Tis a villain, sir,
310 I do not love to look on.

PROSPERO.   But as 'tis,
We cannot miss him. He does make our fire,
Fetch in our wood, and serves in offices
That profit us. What ho! slave! Caliban!
Thou earth, thou! speak.

CALIBAN. [*Within.*]   There's wood enough within.

315 **PROSPERO.**   Come forth, I say, there's other business for
    thee.
Come, thou tortoise, when?

Enter ARIEL *like a water-nymph.*

Fine apparition! My quaint Ariel,
Hark in thine ear.

ARIEL.   My lord, it shall be done.   *Exit.*

PROSPERO.   Thou poisonous slave, got by the devil
    himself
320 Upon thy wicked dam, come forth!

Enter CALIBAN.

CALIBAN.   As wicked dew as e'er my mother brush'd

With raven's feather from unwholesome fen[48]
Drop on you both! A south-west blow on ye,
And blister you all o'er!

325 PROSPERO.   For this, be sure, tonight thou shalt have
     cramps,
Side-stitches, that shall pen thy breath up; urchins[49]
Shall, for that vast of night that they may work,
All exercise on thee; thou shalt be pinch'd
As thick as honeycomb, each pinch more stinging
330 Than bees that made 'em.

CALIBAN.   I must eat my dinner.
This island's mine by Sycorax my mother,
Which thou tak'st from me. When thou cam'st first,
Thou strok'st me and madest much of me, wouldst give
     me
Water with berries in't, and teach me how
335 To name the bigger light, and how the less,
That burn by day and night; and then I lov'd thee
And show'd thee all the qualities o' th' isle,
The fresh springs, brine-pits, barren place and fertile.
Curs'd be I that did so! All the charms
340 Of Sycorax, toads, beetles, bats, light on you!
For I am all the subjects that you have,
Which first was mine own king; and here you sty[50] me
In this hard rock, whiles you do keep from me
The rest o' th' island.

PROSPERO.   Thou most lying slave,
345 Whom stripes[51] may move, not kindness! I have us'd thee
(Filth as thou art) with human care, and lodg'd thee
In mine own cell, till thou didst seek to violate
The honor of my child.

CALIBAN.   O ho, O ho, would't had been done!
350 Thou didst prevent me; I had peopled else
This isle with Calibans.

MIRANDA.   Abhorred slave,
Which any print of goodness wilt not take,
Being capable of all ill! I pitied thee,
Took pains to make thee speak, taught thee each hour
355 One thing or other. When thou didst not, savage,
Know thine own meaning, but wouldst gabble[52] like

◄ What does
Caliban say about
the island?

◄ How did Prospero
once treat Caliban?
What did Caliban do
for Prospero? How
does Prospero treat
Caliban now?

◄ Why did Prospero
begin to treat Caliban
more harshly?

◄ What did
Miranda teach
Caliban?

---

48. **fen.** Swampy land
49. **urchins.** Hedgehogs; evil spirits in the shape of hedgehogs
50. **sty.** Keep, as in a cage or pen
51. **stripes.** Whip lashings
52. **gabble.** Chatter

▶ What does Miranda say about Caliban's "race"?

A thing most brutish, I endow'd thy purposes
With words that made them known. But thy vile race
(Though thou didst learn) had that in't which good
    natures
360 Could not abide to be with; therefore wast thou
Deservedly confined into this rock,
Who hadst deserved more than a prison.

▶ How does Caliban feel about what Miranda has taught him? Why might Caliban find Prospero's and Miranda's teachings unprofitable?

CALIBAN.   You taught me language, and my profit on't
Is, I know how to curse. The red-plague rid you
365 For learning me your language!

PROSPERO.   Hag-seed, hence!
Fetch us in fuel, and be quick, thou'rt best,
To answer other business. Shrug'st thou, malice?
If thou neglect'st or dost unwillingly
What I command, I'll rack thee with old cramps,
370 Fill all thy bones with aches, make thee roar
That beasts shall tremble at thy din.

CALIBAN.   No, pray thee.
[Aside.] I must obey. His art is of such pow'r,
It would control my dam's[53] god, Setebos,[54]
And make a vassal[55] of him.

PROSPERO.   So, slave, hence!
                                    Exit CALIBAN.

Enter FERDINAND; and ARIEL, invisible, playing and singing.

ARIEL'S SONG

375   Come unto these yellow sands,
            And then take hands:
        Curtsied when you have, and kiss'd,
            The wild waves whist:[56]
        Foot it featly[57] here and there,
380   And, sweet sprites, the burthen[58] bear.
        Hark, hark!
                    [Burthen, dispersedly, within.] Bow-wow.
        The watch-dogs bark!
                    [Burthen, dispersedly, within.] Bow-wow.
385   Hark, hark, I hear
        The strain of strutting chanticleer;[59]
                    [Cry, within.] Cock-a-diddle-dow.

53. **dam's.** Mother's
54. **Setebos.** Ancient South American god
55. **vassal.** Servant
56. **whist.** Quieted
57. **Foot it featly.** Move carefully
58. **burthen.** Chorus or refrain of a song
59. **chanticleer.** Rooster

FERDINAND.   Where should this music be? I' th' air, or th'
     earth?
It sounds no more; and sure it waits upon
390 Some god o' th' island. Sitting on a bank,
Weeping again the King my father's wrack,
This music crept by me upon the waters,
Allaying both their fury and my passion
With its sweet air; thence I have follow'd it,
395 Or it hath drawn me rather. But 'tis gone.
No, it begins again.

Why was
Ferdinand weeping?
What was the effect
of Ariel's music on the
storm? on Ferdinand's
emotions?

ARIEL'S SONG

Full fathom five thy father lies,
     Of his bones are coral made:
Those are pearls that were his eyes:
400   Nothing of him that doth fade,
But doth suffer a sea-change
Into something rich and strange.
Sea-nymphs hourly ring his knell.[60]
             [*Burthen, within.*] Ding-dong.
405   Hark! now I hear them—ding-dong bell.

What does Ariel
say about Ferdinand's
father? How has the
sea changed him?

FERDINAND.   The ditty does remember my drown'd
     father.
This is no mortal business, nor no sound
That the earth owes. I hear it now above me.

PROSPERO.   The fringed curtains of thine eye advance,
410 And say what thou seest yond.[61]

MIRANDA.   What, is't a spirit?
Lord, how it looks about! Believe me, sir,
It carries a brave form. But 'tis a spirit.

PROSPERO.   No, wench, it eats and sleeps, and hath
     such senses
As we have—such. This gallant which thou seest
415 Was in the wrack; and, but he's something stain'd
With grief (that's beauty's canker),[62] thou mightst call
     him
A goodly person. He hath lost his fellows,
And strays about to find 'em.

MIRANDA.   I might call him
A thing divine, for nothing natural
420 I ever saw so noble.

What does
Miranda think of
Ferdinand when she
sees him for the first
time?

---

60. **knell.** Sound of a funeral bell
61. **yond.** Beyond; yonder
62. **canker.** Worm that eats and destroys flowers

ACT I, SCENE ii   17

► Is Prospero happy that Miranda finds Ferdinand so pleasing? What do you think Prospero is planning?

► What does Ferdinand think of Miranda when he sees her for the first time?

PROSPERO.   [*Aside.*] It goes on, I see,
As my soul prompts it. Spirit, fine spirit, I'll free thee
Within two days for this.

FERDINAND.   Most sure, the goddess
On whom these airs attend! Vouchsafe[63] my pray'r
May know if you remain upon this island,

425   And that you will some good instruction give
How I may bear me here. My prime request,
Which I do last pronounce, is (O you wonder!)
If you be maid, or no?

MIRANDA.   No wonder, sir;
But certainly a maid.

FERDINAND.   My language? heavens!
430   I am the best of them that speak this speech,
Were I but where 'tis spoken.

PROSPERO.   How? the best?
What wert thou, if the King of Naples heard thee?

FERDINAND.   A single thing, as I am now, that wonders
To hear thee speak of Naples. He does hear me,

435   And that he does I weep. Myself am Naples,[64]
Who with mine eyes (never since at ebb) beheld
The King my father wrack'd.

MIRANDA.   Alack, for mercy!

FERDINAND.   Yes, faith, and all his lords, the Duke of
    Milan
And his brave son being twain.[65]

PROSPERO.   [*Aside.*]   The Duke of Milan
440   And his more braver daughter could control thee,
If now 'twere fit to do't. At the first sight
They have chang'd eyes.[66] Delicate Ariel,
I'll set thee free for this.—A word, good sir,
I fear you have done yourself some wrong; a word.

► How does Miranda feel about Ferdinand?

► How does Ferdinand feel about Miranda?

445   **MIRANDA.**   Why speaks my father so ungently? This
Is the third man that e'er I saw; the first
That e'er I sigh'd for. Pity move my father
To be inclin'd my way!

FERDINAND.   O, if a virgin,
And your affection not gone forth, I'll make you
450   The Queen of Naples.

PROSPERO.   Soft, sir, one word more.

---

63. **Vouchsafe.** Keep safe
64. **Naples.** King of Naples
65. **twain.** Two
66. **changed eyes.** Looked at each other lovingly

[*Aside.*] They are both in either's pow'rs; but this swift
  business
I must uneasy[67] make, lest too light winning
Make the prize light.[68]—One word more: I charge thee
That thou attend me. Thou dost here <u>usurp</u>
455 The name thou ow'st not, and hast put thyself
Upon this island as a spy, to win it
From me, the lord on't.

FERDINAND.   No, as I am a man.

MIRANDA.   There's nothing ill can dwell in such a
  temple.
If the ill spirit have so fair a house,
460 Good things will strive to dwell with't.

PROSPERO.   Follow me.
Speak not you for him; he's a traitor.—Come,
I'll <u>manacle</u> thy neck and feet together.
Sea-water shalt thou drink; thy food shall be
The fresh-brook mussels, wither'd roots, and husks
465 Wherein the acorn cradled. Follow.

FERDINAND.   No,
I will resist such entertainment till
Mine enemy has more pow'r.

                    He draws, and is charmed from moving.

MIRANDA.   O dear father,
Make not too rash a trial of him, for
He's gentle, and not fearful.

PROSPERO.   What, I say,
470 My foot my tutor?[69] Put thy sword up, traitor,
Who mak'st a show but dar'st not strike, thy conscience
Is so possess'd with guilt. Come, from thy ward,
For I can here disarm thee with this stick,
And make thy weapon drop.

MIRANDA.   Beseech you, father.

475 PROSPERO.   Hence! hang not on my garments.

MIRANDA.   Sir, have pity,

◀ *Why does
Prospero treat
Ferdinand harshly
and take him
captive?*

---

67. **uneasy.** Challenging
68. **light.** Little valued; easy
69. **My foot my tutor?** Someone younger presumes to tell me how to behave?

Words
For
Everyday
Use

u • surp (yo͞o zʉrp´) *vt.*, take or assume power by force
man • a • cle (man´ə kəl) *vt.*, restrain by tying or
chaining up

I'll be his surety.

PROSPERO.   Silence! one word more
Shall make me chide thee, if not hate thee. What,
An advocate for an imposter? Hush!
Thou think'st there is no more such shapes as he,
480 Having seen but him and Caliban. Foolish wench,
To the most of men this is a Caliban,
And they to him are angels.

MIRANDA.   My affections
Are then most humble; I have no ambition
To see a goodlier man.

PROSPERO.   [To FERDINAND.] Come on; obey:
485 Thy nerves are in their infancy again
And have no vigor in them.

FERDINAND.   So they are.
My spirits, as in a dream, are all bound up.
My father's loss, the weakness which I feel,
The wrack of all my friends, nor this man's threats,
490 To whom I am subdu'd, are but light to me,
Might I but through my prison once a day
Behold this maid. All corners else o' th' earth
Let liberty make use of; space enough
Have I in such a prison.

PROSPERO.   [Aside.] It works. [To FERDINAND.] Come on.—
495 Thou hast done well, fine Ariel! [To FERDINAND.] Follow
    me.
[To ARIEL.] Hark what thou else shalt do me.

MIRANDA.   Be of comfort.
My father's of a better nature, sir,
Than he appears by speech. This is unwonted[70]
Which now came from him.

PROSPERO.   Thou shalt be as free
500 As mountain winds; but then exactly do
All points of my command.

ARIEL.   To th' syllable.

PROSPERO. [To FERDINAND.] Come, follow. [To MIRANDA.]
    Speak not for him.   Exeunt.

---

70. **unwonted.** Rare, unusual

Responding to the Selection

In small groups, discuss how you feel about Prospero and his powers. Do you admire his powers and think that he has good reasons for acting as he does, do you think he is meddlesome and manipulative, or do you feel some other way about him? What do you think about the way he treats the other people on the island, including Miranda?

Reviewing the Selection

Recalling and Interpreting

1. **R:** Who causes the tempest that threatens the ship at the beginning of act 1? What is the result of this storm for the ship and for its passengers? What do the people aboard the other ships believe has happened?

2. **I:** How does Miranda react to the storm? What do her feelings reveal about her character? What motivates Prospero to have Ariel raise a tempest against this particular ship? What does Prospero hope to accomplish?

3. **R:** What position did Prospero once hold? How did Prospero lose this position? Why are Prospero and Miranda on the island? What did Gonzalo do to help Prospero and Miranda survive?

4. **I:** In what way did Prospero contribute to his own loss of power? Does he accept blame for this loss? Why, or why not?

5. **R:** Why does Ariel serve Prospero? Why does Caliban serve Prospero?

6. **I:** How does Prospero feel about Ariel? about Caliban? How does Ariel regard serving Prospero? How does Caliban regard serving Prospero?

7. **R:** What does Miranda think of Ferdinand when she sees him for the first time? What does Ferdinand think of Miranda? What does Prospero do to Ferdinand?

8. **I:** Why do Miranda and Ferdinand each think that the other cannot be a mortal? Why does Prospero treat Ferdinand harshly?

Synthesizing

9. What is Prospero's "art"? Compare and contrast Prospero's art to Sycorax's magic. Of what is Prospero's art a result? What does Prospero control with his art?

10. In what way has the relationship between Prospero and Caliban changed since Prospero first came to the island? Why does Prospero treat Caliban harshly now? How does Caliban feel about his position on the island? How does Prospero feel about his position on the island? Who do you believe is in the right?

Understanding Literature (QUESTIONS FOR DISCUSSION)

1. Character and Anagram. A **character** is a person (or sometimes an animal) who figures in the action of a literary work. An **anagram** is a word or phrase created by rearranging the letters of a word or phrase. One of Shakespeare's sources for *The Tempest* was Michel de Montaigne's essay "Of Cannibals" (see page 110). In this essay, Montaigne argues that the indigenous inhabitants of the New World, though often seen as barbarous by Europeans, were more humane, more natural, and in many ways superior to Europeans. Of what word is Caliban's name an anagram? In what way might Caliban's character represent Shakespeare's response to Montaigne's elevation of "natural" society? Does Shakespeare present Caliban as a "noble savage" or as something else? In your discussion, focus on the description of Caliban in the list of dramatis personae, other characters' descriptions of Caliban, and Caliban's own words and deeds.

2. Scene and Setting. A **scene** is a short section of a literary work that presents action that occurs in a single place or at a single time. The **setting** of a literary work is the time and place in which it occurs, together with all the details used to create a sense of a particular time and place. Where is act I, scene i set? In what way is nature portrayed in this scene? Scenes such as act I, scene i are sometimes called *window scenes* in the study of Shakespeare because, like windows, such scenes allow some light to be shed upon the action of the play. Window scenes often involve minor characters, such as the ship-master, boatswain, and mariners in act I, scene i, who do not figure in the action of the rest of the play. These characters typically comment on the social or political climate in which the play is situated. In act I, scene i, what does the boatswain reveal about the limits of political authority? In the boatswain's view, what is more powerful, nature or humans? In what way is this view of nature undercut when the cause of the storm is revealed?

3. Theme. A **theme** is a central idea in a literary work. Shakespeare's dramas, especially his romances, are filled with songs. These songs serve more than one purpose—in addition to entertaining music-loving Elizabethan and Jacobean audiences, they also comment upon the play's action or focus on a certain theme. Ariel's song "Full fathom five thy father lies" in act I, scene ii focuses upon a theme central to many of Shakespeare's romances—transformation. What is being transformed in this song and in what way? How does this theme of magical transformation relate to what Prospero is attempting to accomplish?

Act II

SCENE i: **Another part of the island.**

Enter ALONSO, SEBASTIAN, ANTONIO, GONZALO, ADRIAN,
FRANCISCO, *and* OTHERS

GONZALO.   Beseech[1] you, sir, be merry; you have cause
(So have we all) of joy; for our escape
Is much beyond our loss. Our hint of woe[2]
Is common: every day some sailor's wife,
5   The masters of some merchant, and the merchant[3]
Have just our theme of woe; but for the miracle
(I mean our preservation), few in millions
Can speak like us. Then wisely, good sir, weigh
Our sorrow with our comfort.

ALONSO.   Prithee, peace.

10   SEBASTIAN.   He receives comfort like cold porridge.

ANTONIO.   The visitor[4] will not give him o'er so.

SEBASTIAN.   Look, he's winding up the watch of his wit;
by and by it will strike.

GONZALO.   Sir—

15   SEBASTIAN.   One. Tell.

GONZALO.   When every grief is entertain'd that's offer'd,
Comes to the entertainer—[5]

SEBASTIAN.   A dollar.

GONZALO.   Dolor[6] comes to him indeed, you have
20   spoken truer than you <u>purpos'd</u>.

SEBASTIAN.   You have taken it wiselier than I meant you
should.

◀ *According to
Gonzalo, why should
the nobles and lords
be "merry"?*

ACT II, SCENE i
1. **Beseech.** I beg
2. **hint of woe.** Occasion of sadness
3. **masters of some merchant, and the merchant.** Captains of a merchant
ship and the owner of the ship
4. **visitor.** One who gives comfort
5. **entertainer.** Griever
6. **Dolor.** Sadness

**Words
For
Everyday
Use**

pur • pos • ed (pʉr′pəs′d) *vt.,* intended

▶ In what way do Antonio and Sebastian react to Gonzalo's positive attitude?

GONZALO.   Therefore, my lord—

ANTONIO.   Fie, what a spendthrift is he of his tongue!

25 ALONSO.   I prithee spare.

GONZALO.   Well, I have done. But yet—

SEBASTIAN.   He will be talking.

ANTONIO.   Which, of he or Adrian, for a good wager, first begins to crow?

30 SEBASTIAN.   The old cock.

ANTONIO.   The cock'rel.

SEBASTIAN.   Done. The wager?

ANTONIO.   A laughter.[7]

SEBASTIAN.   A match!

35 ADRIAN.   Though this island seem to be desert[8]—

SEBASTIAN.   Ha, ha, ha!

ANTONIO.   So: you're paid!

ADRIAN.   Uninhabitable, and almost inaccessible—

SEBASTIAN.   Yet—

40 ADRIAN.   Yet—

ANTONIO.   He could not miss't.

ADRIAN.   It must needs be of subtle, tender, and delicate temperance.

ANTONIO.   Temperance was a delicate wench.

45 SEBASTIAN.   Ay, and a subtle, as he most learnedly deliver'd.

▶ In what way do Gonzalo and Adrian perceive the island? In what way do Antonio and Sebastian perceive the island?

ADRIAN.   The air breathes upon us here most sweetly.

SEBASTIAN.   As if it had lungs, and rotten ones.

ANTONIO.   Or, as 'twere perfum'd by a fen.[9]

50 GONZALO.   Here is every thing advantageous to life.

ANTONIO.   True, save means to live.

SEBASTIAN.   Of that there's none, or little.

GONZALO.   How lush and lusty the grass looks! How green!

---

7. **A laughter.** A good laugh (The winner will have a good laugh on the loser.)
8. **desert.** Deserted
9. **fen.** Swamp

55   ANTONIO.   The ground indeed is tawny.[10]

      SEBASTIAN.   With an eye of green in't.

      ANTONIO.   He misses not much.

      SEBASTIAN.   No; he doth but mistake the truth totally.

      GONZALO.   But the rareity of it is—which is indeed
60 almost beyond credit—

      SEBASTIAN.   As many vouch'd[11] rareities are.

      GONZALO.   That our garments, being (as they were)
drench'd in the sea, hold notwithstanding their
freshness and glosses, being rather new dyed than
65 stained with salt water.

      ANTONIO.   If but one of his pockets could speak, would
it not say he lies?

      SEBASTIAN.   Ay, or very falsely pocket up his report.

      GONZALO.   Methinks our garments are now as fresh as
70 when we put them on first in Afric,[12] at the marriage of
the King's fair daughter Claribel to the King of Tunis.[13]

      SEBASTIAN.   'Twas a sweet marriage, and we prosper well
in our return.

      ADRIAN.   Tunis was never grac'd before with such a
75 paragon to their queen.

      GONZALO.   Not since widow Dido's[14] time.

      ANTONIO.   Widow! a pox o'[15] that! How came that
widow in? Widow Dido!

      SEBASTIAN.   What if he had said "widower Æneas"[16]
80 too? Good Lord, how you take it!

◄ *What does
Gonzalo note about
the group's clothing?
What do Antonio and
Sebastian think about
his observation?*

◄ *From what wed-
ding is the group of
nobles returning?*

---

10. **tawny.** Brownish yellow
11. **vouch'd.** True
12. **Afric.** Africa
13. **Tunis.** Capital of Tunisia, located in northern Africa
14. **Dido's.** Dido is the founder and widowed queen of Carthage who falls in
love with the Roman hero Aeneas and kills herself when he leaves her.
15. **a pox o'.** A pox on; curse
16. **Æneas.** Roman hero of the *Aeneid*; traditionally, although not historically,
the founder of Rome

**Words
For
Everyday
Use**   **par • a • gon** (par´ə gän´) *n.*, model of perfection or
excellence

ADRIAN. "Widow Dido," said you? You make me study of that. She was of Carthage,[17] not of Tunis.

GONZALO. This Tunis, sir, was Carthage.

ADRIAN. Carthage?

85 GONZALO. I assure you, Carthage.

ANTONIO. His word is more than the miraculous harp.[18]

SEBASTIAN. He hath rais'd the wall, and houses too.

ANTONIO. What impossible matter will he make easy
90 next?

SEBASTIAN. I think he will carry this island home in his pocket, and give it his son for an apple.

ANTONIO. And sowing the kernels[19] of it in the sea, bring forth more islands.

95 GONZALO. Ay.

ANTONIO. Why, in good time.

GONZALO. Sir, we were talking that our garments seem now as fresh as when we were at Tunis at the marriage of your daughter, who is now queen.

100 ANTONIO. And the rarest that e'er came there.

SEBASTIAN. Bate,[20] I beseech you, widow Dido.

ANTONIO. O, widow Dido! Ay, widow Dido.

GONZALO. Is not, sir, my doublet[21] as fresh as the first day I wore it? I mean, in a sort.

105 ANTONIO. That "sort" was well fish'd for.

GONZALO. When I wore it at your daughter's marriage?

▶ Why doesn't Alonso care about Gonzalo's observation?

ALONSO. You cram these words into mine ears against
The stomach of my sense.[22] Would I had never
Married my daughter there! For, coming thence,
110 My son is lost and (in my rate) she too,
Who is so far from Italy removed
I ne'er again shall see her. O thou mine heir

---

17. **Carthage.** Ancient city in north Africa, near Tunis
18. **miraculous harp.** Ovid tells how Amphion created the walls of the city of Thebes by playing a harp. Gonzalo has created a whole new city with his words.
19. **kernels.** Seeds
20. **Bate.** Except
21. **doublet.** Close-fitting jacket
22. **against . . . sense.** Against my better judgment

Of Naples and of Milan, what strange fish
Hath made his meal on thee?[23]

FRANCISCO.   Sir, he may live.
115 I saw him beat the surges under him,
And ride upon their backs. He trod the water,
Whose <u>enmity</u> he flung aside, and breasted
The surge most swol'n that met him. His bold head
'Bove the <u>contentious</u> waves he kept, and oared
120 Himself with his good arms in lusty stroke
To th' shore, that o'er his wave-worn basis[24] bowed,
As stooping to relieve him. I not doubt
He came alive to land.

ALONSO.   No, no, he's gone.

SEBASTIAN.   Sir, you may thank yourself for this great
     loss,
125 That would not bless our Europe with your daughter,
But rather lose her to an African,
Where she, at least, is banish'd from your eye,
Who hath cause to wet the grief[25] on't.

ALONSO.   Prithee, peace.

SEBASTIAN.   You were kneel'd to, and <u>importun'd</u>
     otherwise
130 By all of us, and the fair soul herself
Weigh'd between loathness[26] and obedience, at
Which end o' th' beam should bow. We have lost your
     son,
I fear, for ever. Milan and Naples have
Moe widows in them of this business' making
135 Than we bring men to comfort them,
The fault's your own.

ALONSO.   So is the dear'st o' th' loss.

GONZALO.   My Lord Sebastian,
The truth you speak doth lack some gentleness,

▶ What does
Francisco say about
Ferdinand?

◀ What does
Sebastian do instead
of comforting his
brother the king for
his loss?

◀ What does
Gonzalo point out
about Sebastian's
manner of speech?

---

23. **what strange . . . thee.** What happened to you? (Alonso is addressing his
son, Ferdinand, whom he assumes has drowned.)
24. **wave-worn basis.** Beach worn by waves
25. **wet the grief.** Cry
26. **weigh'd between loathness.** Torn between reluctance

Words For Everyday Use	en • mi • ty (en´mə tē) n., hostility
	con • ten • tious (kən ten´shəs) adj., argumentative
	im • por • tuned (im´pôr tōōn´d) vt., asked for urgently; demanded of

And time to speak it in. You rub the sore,
140 When you should bring the plaster.

SEBASTIAN.   Very well.

ANTONIO.   And most chirurgeonly.[27]

GONZALO.   It is foul weather in us all, good sir,
When you are cloudy.

SEBASTIAN.   Fowl weather?

ANTONIO.   Very foul.

GONZALO.   Had I plantation[28] of this isle, my lord—

145 ANTONIO.   He'd sow't with nettle-seed.

SEBASTIAN.   Or docks, or
        mallows.[29]

GONZALO.   And were the king on't, what would I do?

SEBASTIAN.   Scape being drunk for want of wine.

GONZALO.   I' th' commonwealth I would, by
        contraries[30]
Execute all things; for no kind of traffic[31]
150 Would I admit; no name of magistrate;
Letters should not be known; riches, poverty,
And use of service, none; contract, succession,
Bourn,[32] bound of land, tilth,[33] vineyard, none;
No use of metal, corn, or wine, or oil;
155 No occupation, all men idle, all;
And women too, but innocent and pure;
No sovereignty—

SEBASTIAN.   Yet he would be king on't.

ANTONIO.   The latter end of his commonwealth forgets
the beginning.

160 GONZALO.   All things in common nature should
        produce

▶ What does
Gonzalo say he
would do if he were
king of the island?
What do Sebastian
and Antonio point
out about Gonzalo's
idea? What do you
think of Gonzalo's
idea? Does it sound
like a perfect world
to you?

---

27. **chirurgeonly.** Like a surgeon or doctor
28. **plantation.** Ownership
29. **mallow.** Marsh plant
30. **contraries.** Opposite of the usual manner
31. **traffic.** Trade
32. **Bourn.** Land boundary
33. **tilth.** Farming

Words For Everyday Use	**sov • er • eign • ty** (säv´rən tē) *n.*, sovereign state or governmental unit

Without sweat or endeavor: treason, felony,
Sword, pike, knife, gun, or need of any engine,
Would I not have; but nature should bring forth,
Of its own kind, all foison,[34] all abundance,
165 To feed my innocent people.

SEBASTIAN.   No marrying 'mong his subjects?

ANTONIO.   None, man; all idle—whores and knaves.

GONZALO.   I would with such perfection govern, sir,
T' excel the golden age.

SEBASTIAN.   'Save his Majesty!

170 ANTONIO.   Long live Gonzalo!

GONZALO.   And—do you mark me,
sir?

ALONSO.   Prithee, no more: thou dost talk nothing to
me.

GONZALO.   I do well believe your Highness; and did it to
minister occasion[35] to these gentlemen, who are of such
175 sensible and nimble lungs that they always use to laugh
at nothing.

ANTONIO.   'Twas you we laugh'd at.

GONZALO.   Who, in this kind of merry fooling, am
nothing to you; so you may continue, and laugh at
180 nothing still.

ANTONIO.   What a blow was there given!

SEBASTIAN.   And[36] it had not fall'n flat-long.[37]

GONZALO.   You are gentlemen of brave mettle; you
would lift the moon out of her sphere, if she would
185 continue in it five weeks without changing.

Enter ARIEL, *invisible, playing solemn music.*

SEBASTIAN.   We would so, and then go a-batfowling.[38]

ANTONIO.   Nay, good my lord, be not angry.

GONZALO.   No, I warrant you, I will not adventure my
discretion[39] so weakly. Will you laugh me asleep, for I
190 am very heavy?

---

34. **foison.** Plenty
35. **minister occasion.** Provide opportunity
36. **And.** If
37. **flat-long.** On the flat part of the sword
38. **a-batfowling.** Bird hunting, usually with sticks
39. **adventure . . . weakly.** Risk my reputation so easily

200   **ANTONIO.**   Go sleep, and hear us.

All sleep except ALONSO, SEBASTIAN, *and* ANTONIO.

ALONSO.   What, all so soon asleep! I wish mine eyes
Would, with themselves, shut up my thoughts. I find
They are inclin'd to do so.

SEBASTIAN.   Please you, sir,
195   Do not omit the heavy offer[40] of it.
It seldom visits sorrow; when it doth,
It is a comforter.

ANTONIO.   We two, my lord,
Will guard your person while you take your rest,
And watch your safety.

ALONSO.   Thank you. Wondrous heavy.

                    ALONSO *sleeps. Exit* ARIEL.

▶ *Who or what causes the group of nobles, with the exception of Antonio and Sebastian, to fall asleep?*

200   **SEBASTIAN.**   What a strange drowsiness possesses them!

ANTONIO.   It is the quality o' th' climate.

SEBASTIAN.   Why
Doth it not then our eyelids sink? I find not
Myself dispos'd to sleep.

ANTONIO.   Nor I, my spirits are nimble.
They fell together all, as by consent;
205   They dropp'd, as by a thunder-stroke. What might.
Worthy Sebastian, O, what might—? No more—
And yet methinks I see it in thy face,
What thou shouldst be. Th' occasion speaks thee, and
My strong imagination sees a crown
210   Dropping upon thy head.

SEBASTIAN.   What? art thou waking?

ANTONIO.   Do you not hear me speak?

SEBASTIAN.   I do, and surely
It is a sleepy language, and thou speak'st
Out of thy sleep. What is it thou didst say?
This is a strange <u>repose</u>, to be asleep

▶ *What does Antonio suggest that Sebastian might one day wear?*

---

40. **omit the heavy offer.** Let the opportunity for sleep pass

Words For Everyday Use   **re • pose** (ri pōz´) *n.*, rest; peace

215   With eyes wide open—standing, speaking, moving—
       And yet so fast asleep.

       ANTONIO.   Noble Sebastian,
       Thou let'st thy fortune sleep—die, rather; wink'st
       Whiles thou art waking.

       SEBASTIAN.   Thou dost snore distinctly,
       There's meaning in thy snores.

◄ What does
Antonio say
Sebastian is doing?

220 ANTONIO.   I am more serious than my custom: you
       Must be so too, if heed me; which to do,
       Trebles thee o'er.[41]

       SEBASTIAN.   Well; I am standing water.[42]

       ANTONIO.   I'll teach you how to flow.

       SEBASTIAN.   Do so. To ebb[43]
       Hereditary sloth instructs me.

       ANTONIO.   O,

225 If you but knew how you the purpose cherish
       Whiles thus you mock it! how, in stripping it,
       You more invest it! Ebbing men, indeed,
       Most often, do so near the bottom run
       By their own fear or sloth.

       SEBASTIAN.   Prithee say on.
230 The setting of thine eye and cheek proclaim
       A matter from thee; and a birth, indeed
       Which throes[44] thee much to yield.

       ANTONIO.   Thus, sir:
       Although this lord of weak remembrance, this
       Who shall be of as little memory
235 When he is earth'd,[45] hath here almost persuaded
       (For he's a spirit of persuasion, only
       Professes to persuade) the King his son's alive,
       'Tis as impossible that he's undrown'd,
       As he that sleeps here swims.

       SEBASTIAN.   I have no hope
240 That he's undrown'd.

       ANTONIO.   O, out of that no hope
       What great hope have you! No hope, that way, is
       Another way so high a hope that even

◄ According to
Antonio, who is no
longer an obstacle to
the throne?

---

41. **Trebles thee o'er.** Increases your wealth
42. **standing water.** Going nowhere
43. **ebb.** Lessen; weaken
44. **throes.** Pain
45. **earth'd.** Buried; dead

Ambition cannot pierce a wink beyond,[46]
But doubt discovery there. Will you grant with me
245 That Ferdinand is drown'd?

SEBASTIAN.   He's gone.

ANTONIO.   Then, tell me,
Who's the next heir of Naples?

SEBASTIAN.   Claribel.

ANTONIO.   She that is Queen of Tunis; she that dwells
Ten leagues beyond man's life;[47] she that from Naples
Can have no note, unless the sun were post—
250 The Man i' the Moon's too slow—till new-born chins
Be rough and razorable; she that from whom
We all were sea-swallow'd, though some cast again
(And by that destiny) to perform an act
Whereof what's past is prologue, what to come
255 In yours and my discharge.

SEBASTIAN.   What stuff is this! How say
    you?
'Tis true, my brother's daughter's Queen of Tunis,
So is she heir of Naples; 'twixt which regions
There is some space.

ANTONIO.   A space whose ev'ry cubit[48]
Seems to cry out, "How shall that Claribel
260 Measure us[49] back to Naples? Keep in Tunis,
And let Sebastian wake." Say, this were death
That now hath seiz'd them, why, they were no worse
Than now they are. There be that can rule Naples
As well as he that sleeps; lords that can prate[50]
265 As amply and unnecessarily
As this Gonzalo; I myself could make
A chough[51] of as deep chat. O that you bore
The mind that I do! What a sleep were this
For your advancement! Do you understand me?

270 SEBASTIAN.   Methinks I do.

ANTONIO.   And how does your
    content
Tender[52] your own good fortune?

► According to Antonio, why is Claribel not a possible contender for the throne of Naples?

► What is Antonio suggesting that Sebastian do? In what way is Antonio speaking from experience?

---

46. **pierce . . . beyond.** Go beyond; overcome
47. **Ten leagues . . . life.** Too far away to matter
48. **cubit.** Ancient unit of linear measure; equal to about 20 inches
49. **Measure us.** Travel the long distance
50. **prate.** Speak foolishly
51. **chough.** Crow
52. **Tender.** Regard

SEBASTIAN. I remember
You did supplant your brother Prospero.

ANTONIO. True.
And look how well my garments sit upon me,
Much feater[53] than before. My brother's servants
275 Were then my fellows, now they are my men.

SEBASTIAN. But, for your conscience?

ANTONIO. Ay, sir; where lies that? if 'twere a kibe,'[54]
'Twould put me to[55] my slipper; but I feel not
This deity in my bosom. Twenty consciences,
280 That stand 'twixt me and Milan, candied be they,
And melt ere[56] they molest! Here lies your brother,
No better than the earth he lies upon,
If he were that which now he's like—that's dead;
Whom I, with this obedient steel, three inches of it,
285 Can lay to bed for ever; whiles you, doing thus,
To the perpetual wink[57] for aye[58] might put
This ancient morsel, this Sir Prudence, who
Should not upbraid our course. For all the rest,
They'll take suggestion as a cat laps milk;
290 They'll tell the clock to[59] any business that
We say befits the hour.

SEBASTIAN. Thy case, dear friend,
Shall be my president:[60] as thou got'st Milan,
I'll come by Naples. Draw thy sword. One stroke
Shall free thee from the tribute which thou payest;
295 And I the King shall love thee.

ANTONIO. Draw together;
And when I rear[61] my hand, do you the like,
To fall it on Gonzalo.

SEBASTIAN. O, but one word. *They talk apart.*

Enter ARIEL *[invisible], with music and song.*

ARIEL. My master through his art foresees the danger
That you, his friend, are in; and sends me forth
300 (For else his project dies) to keep them living.

◄ *How does Antonio feel about supplanting his brother Prospero? Does he have any regrets?*

◄ *What does Antonio say he will do for Sebastian? What does he ask Sebastian to do?*

◄ *What will Sebastian do for Antonio if he kills Alonso?*

◄ *Who is about to stop Antonio's scheme? Why has Prospero intervened in this way?*

---

53. **feater.** More gracefully
54. **kibe.** Painful swelling caused by the cold
55. **put me to.** Make me wear
56. **ere.** Before
57. **perpetual wink.** Perpetual sleep, i.e. death
58. **aye.** Always
59. **tell the clock to.** Act punctually upon
60. **president.** Precedent, example
61. **rear.** Raise

While you here do snoring lie,
Open-ey'd conspiracy
His time doth take.
If of life you keep a care,
305   Shake off slumber, and beware.
Awake, awake!

ANTONIO.   Then let us both be sudden.

GONZALO.   [*Waking.*]   Now, good
angels
Preserve the King.   *Wakes* ALONSO.

ALONSO.   Why, how now, ho! Awake? Why are you
drawn?
310 Wherefore this ghastly looking?

GONZALO.   What's the matter?

▶ *What reason does Sebastian give for his and Antonio's drawn swords?*

SEBASTIAN.   Whiles we stood here securing your repose,
Even now, we heard a hollow burst of bellowing
Like bulls, or rather lions. Did't not wake you?
It strook mine ear most terribly.

ALONSO.   I heard nothing.

315 ANTONIO.   O, 'twas a din[62] to fright a monster's ear,
To make an earthquake; sure, it was the roar
Of a whole herd of lions.

ALONSO.   Heard you this, Gonzalo?

GONZALO.   Upon mine honor, sir, I heard a humming,
(And that a strange one too) which did awake me.
320 I shak'd you, sir, and cried. As mine eyes open'd,
I saw their weapons drawn. There was a noise,
That's verily.[63] 'Tis best we stand upon our guard,
Or that we quit this place. Let's draw our weapons.

ALONSO.   Lead off this ground, and let's make further
search
325 For my poor son.

GONZALO.   Heavens keep him from these beasts!
For he is sure, i' th' island.

ALONSO.   Lead away.

ARIEL.   Prospero my lord shall know what I have done.
So, King, go safely on to seek thy son.   *Exeunt.*

---

62. **din.** Loud noise
63. **verily.** True; for sure

SCENE ii: **Another part of the island.**

Enter CALIBAN *with a burthen of wood. A noise of thunder heard.*

CALIBAN.   All the infections that the sun sucks up
From bogs, fens, flats, on Prosper fall, and make him
By inch-meal[1] a disease! His spirits hear me,
And yet I needs must curse. But they'll nor pinch,
5   Fright me with urchin-shows,[2] pitch me i' the mire,
Nor lead me, like a fire-brand,[3] in the dark
Out of my way, unless he bid 'em; but
For every trifle are they set upon me,
Sometime like apes that mow[4] and chatter at me,
10   And after bite me; then like hedgehogs which
Lie tumbling in my barefoot way, and mount
Their pricks[5] at my footfall; sometime am I
All wound with adders,[6] who with cloven tongues
Do hiss me into madness.
Enter TRINCULO.

                              Lo, now, lo,
15   Here comes a spirit of his, and to torment me
For bringing wood in slowly. I'll fall flat,
Perchance[7] he will not mind me.

TRINCULO.   Here's neither bush nor shrub to bear off
any weather at all, and another storm brewing, I hear it
20   sing i' th' wind. Yond[8] same black cloud, yond huge
one, looks like a foul bumbard[9] that would shed his
liquor. If it should thunder as it did before, I know not
where to hide my head. Yond same cloud cannot choose
but fall by pailfuls. What have we here? a man
25   or a fish? dead or alive? A fish, he smells like a fish; a
very ancient and fish-like smell; a kind of, not of the
newest poor-John.[10] A strange fish! Were I in England
now (as once I was) and had but this fish painted,[11] not
a holiday fool there but would give a piece of silver.

◄ *Why does
Caliban curse
Prospero? In what
way does Prospero
torture Caliban?*

◄ *What does
Trinculo see? For
what does Trinculo
mistake this person?*

◄ *What does
Trinculo say about
the English people?*

ACT II, SCENE ii
  1. **by inch-meal.** Inch by inch; slowly
  2. **urchin-shows.** Sightings of goblins in the shape of hedgehogs
  3. **fire-brand.** Ghostly light; will'o-the-wisp
  4. **mow.** Mock by making faces
  5. **pricks.** Quills of the hedgehogs
  6. **adders.** Snakes
  7. **Perchance.** Perhaps
  8. **Yond.** Beyond
  9. **bumbard.** Leather jug
 10. **poor-John.** Dried, salted fish
 11. **painted.** On a sign at a fair to attract the curious

30   There would this monster make a man; any strange
      beast there makes a man. When they will not give a
      doit[12] to relieve a lame beggar, they will lay out ten to
      see a dead Indian. Legg'd like a man; and his fins like
      arms! Warm, o' my troth![13] I do now let loose my
35   opinion, hold it no longer: this is no fish, but an
      islander, that hath lately suffer'd by a thunderbolt.

► What does
Trinculo do to escape
the storm?

      [*Thunder.*] Alas, the storm is come again! My best way is
      to creep under his gaberdine;[14] there is no other shelter
      hereabout. Misery acquaints a man with strange
40   bedfellows. I will here shroud till the dregs of the storm
      be past.

Enter STEPHANO, *singing, a bottle in his hand.*

STEPHANO. "I shall no more to sea, to sea,
                Here shall I die ashore—"

      This is a very scurvy[15] tune to sing at a man's funeral.
45   Well, here's my comfort.   *Drinks. (Sings.)*

          "The master, the swabber,[16] the boatswain, and I,
                The gunner[17] and his mate,
            Lov'd Mall, Meg, and Marian, and Margery,
                But none of us car'd for Kate;
50   For she had a tongue with a tang,
                Would cry to a sailor, 'Go hang!'
            She lov'd not the savor of tar nor of pitch,
            Yet a tailor might scratch her where she did itch.
                Then to sea, boys, and let her go hang!"

55   This is a scurvy tune too; but here's my comfort.
                                                    Drinks.

CALIBAN.   Do not torment me! O!

STEPHANO.   What's the matter? Have we devils here? Do
      you put tricks upon 's[18] with savages and men of
      Inde?[19] Ha? I have not scap'd[20] drowning to be afeard
60   now of your four legs; for it hath been said, "As proper a
      man as ever went on four legs cannot make him give
      ground"; and it shall be said so again while Stephano
      breathes at' nostrils.

---

12. **doit.** Coin of little value
13. **troth.** Faith
14. **gaberdine.** Coat
15. **scurvy.** Foul
16. **swabber.** Person who mops the deck of a ship
17. **gunner.** Person who mans the cannon or guns of a ship
18. **upon 's.** Upon us
19. **Inde.** India
20. **scap'd.** Escaped

CALIBAN.   The spirit torments me! O!

65 STEPHANO.   This is some monster of the isle with four
legs, who hath got (as I take it) an ague.[21] Where the
devil should he learn our language? I will give him some
relief, if it be but for that. If I can recover him, and keep
him tame, and get to Naples with him, he's a present for
70 any emperor that ever trod on neat's-leather.[22]

CALIBAN.   Do not torment me, prithee. I'll bring my
wood home faster.

STEPHANO.   He's in his fit now, and does not talk after
the wisest. He shall taste of my bottle; if he have never
75 drunk wine afore,[23] it will go near to remove his fit. If I
can recover him, and keep him tame, I will not take too
much for him; he shall pay for him that hath him, and
that soundly.

CALIBAN.   Thou dost[24] me yet but little hurt; thou wilt
80 anon,[25] I know it by thy trembling. Now Prosper works
upon thee.

STEPHANO.   Come on your ways. Open your mouth;
here is that which will give language to you, cat.[26] Open
your mouth; this will shake your shaking, I can tell you,
85 and that soundly. You cannot tell who's your friend.
Open your chaps[27] again.

CALIBAN *drinks.*

TRINCULO.   I should know that voice; it should be—but
he is drown'd; and these are devils: O, defend me!

STEPHANO.   Four legs and two voices; a most delicate
90 monster! His forward voice now is to speak well of his
friend; his backward voice is to utter foul speeches and
to detract. If all the wine in my bottle will recover him, I
will help his ague. Come.
[CALIBAN *drinks again.*] Amen! I will pour some in thy
95 other mouth.

TRINCULO.   Stephano!

STEPHANO.   Doth thy other mouth call me? Mercy,
mercy! This is a devil, and no monster: I will leave him,

◀ For what does
Stephano mistake
Caliban and
Trinculo? What does
Stephano say he
plans to do with this
creature?

◀ What does
Stephano think when
he hears Trinculo's
voice?

---

21. **ague.** Fever
22. **neat's-leather.** Cowhide
23. **afore.** Before
24. **dost.** Do
25. **anon.** Soon
26. **here is . . . you cat.** From the saying "Liquor will make a cat speak"
27. **chaps.** Jaws

I have no long spoon.[28]

100   **TRINCULO.**   Stephano! If thou beest Stephano, touch
me, and speak to me; for I am Trinculo—be not afeard—
thy good friend Trinculo.

STEPHANO.   If thou beest Trinculo, come forth. I'll pull
thee by the lesser legs. If any be Trinculo's legs, these are
105   they. Thou art very Trinculo indeed! How camest thou
to be the siege[29] of this moon-calf?[30] Can he vent[31]
Trinculos?

TRINCULO.   I took him to be kill'd with a thunder-
stroke. But art thou not drown'd, Stephano? I hope now
110   thou art not drown'd. Is the storm overblown? I hid me
under the dead moon-calf's gaberdine for fear of the
storm. And art thou living, Stephano? O Stephano, two
Neapolitans scap'd!

STEPHANO.   Prithee do not turn me about, my stomach
115   is not constant.[32]

► For what does
Caliban mistake
Trinculo and
Stephano?

CALIBAN.   [*Aside.*] These be fine things, and if[33] they be
not sprites.[34] That's a brave god, and bears celestial
liquor. I will kneel to him.

STEPHANO.   How didst thou scape? How cam'st thou
120   hither? Swear by this bottle how thou cam'st hither—I
escap'd upon a butt of sack[35] which the sailors heav'd
o'erboard—by this bottle, which I made of the bark of a
tree with mine own hands since I was cast ashore.

► To whom does
Caliban swear alle-
giance? Why?

CALIBAN.   I'll swear upon that bottle to be thy true
125   subject, for the liquor is not earthly.

STEPHANO.   Here; swear then how thou escap'dst.

TRINCULO.   Swom ashore, man, like a duck. I can swim
like a duck, I'll be sworn.

STEPHANO.   Here, kiss the book.[36] [*Passing the bottle.*]
130   Though thou canst swim like a duck, thou art made like
a goose.[37]

---

28. **long spoon.** From the saying "He that eats with the devil must have a long spoon"
29. **siege.** Excrement
30. **moon-calf.** Creature born deformed because of the moon's influence
31. **vent.** Give off, emit
32. **constant.** Well
33. **and if.** If
34. **sprites.** Spirits
35. **butt of sack.** Barrel of wine
36. **kiss the book.** Take a drink from the bottle
37. **made like a goose.** Silly

TRINCULO. O Stephano, hast any more of this?

STEPHANO. The whole butt, man. My cellar is in a rock by the sea-side, where my wine is hid. How now, moon-
135 calf? how does thine ague?

CALIBAN. Hast thou not dropp'd from heaven?

STEPHANO. Out o' the moon, I do assure thee. I was the Man i' th' Moon when time was.

CALIBAN. I have seen thee in her, and I do adore thee.
140 My mistress show'd me thee, and thy dog, and thy bush.

STEPHANO. Come, swear to that; kiss the book. I will furnish it anon with new contents. Swear.

CALIBAN *drinks.*

TRINCULO. By this good light, this is a very shallow
145 monster! I afeard of him? A very weak monster! The Man i' th' Moon! A most poor <u>credulous</u> monster! Well drawn,[38] monster, in good sooth![39]

CALIBAN. I'll show thee every fertile inch o' th' island; And I will kiss thy foot: I prithee be my god.

150 **TRINCULO.** By this light, a most <u>perfidious</u> and drunken monster! When 's god's asleep, he'll rob his bottle.

CALIBAN. I'll kiss thy foot; I'll swear myself thy subject.

STEPHANO. Come on then; down, and swear.

155 **TRINCULO.** I shall laugh myself to death at this puppy-headed monster. A most scurvy monster! I could find in my heart to beat him—

STEPHANO. Come, kiss.

TRINCULO. But that the poor monster's in drink. An
160 abominable monster!

CALIBAN. I'll show thee the best springs; I'll pluck thee berries;
I'll fish for thee, and get thee wood enough.
A plague upon the tyrant that I serve!

◀ *What does Stephano say he is? What is Caliban's reaction to this statement?*

◀ *What does Caliban ask of Stephano?*

◀ *Does Caliban expect to be accepted as an equal or as a friend to Stephano, or does he believe that he must serve him as a slave as he has served Prospero and Miranda?*

---

38. **well drawn.** A good long drink you've taken
39. **sooth.** Truth

Words For Everyday Use	**cred • u • lous** (krej´o͞o ləs) *adj.*, easily convinced **per • fid • i • ous** (pər fid´ē əs) *adj.*, treacherous; faithless

I'll bear him no more sticks, but follow thee,
165 Thou wondrous man.

TRINCULO.   A most ridiculous monster, to make a
wonder of a poor drunkard!

CALIBAN.   I prithee, let me bring thee where crabs[40]
grow;
And I with my long nails will dig thee pig-nuts;[41]
170 Show thee a jay's nest and instruct thee how
To snare the nimble marmozet;[42] I'll bring thee
To clust'ring filberts[43] and sometimes I'll get thee
Young scamels[44] from the rock. Wilt thou go with me?

STEPHANO.   I prithee now lead the way without any
175 more talking. Trinculo, the King and all our company
else being drown'd, we will inherit here. Here! bear my
bottle. Fellow Trinculo, we'll fill him by and by again.

CALIBAN.   [Sings drunkenly.] Farewell, master; farewell,
farewell!

TRINCULO.   A howling monster; a drunken monster!

180 CALIBAN.   No more dams I'll make for fish
Nor fetch in firing
At requiring;
Nor scrape trenchering[45], nor wash dish
'Ban, 'Ban, Ca-Caliban
185 Has a new master, get a new man.
Freedom, high-day! High-day, freedom! freedom,
high-day, freedom!

STEPHANO.   O brave monster! lead the way.

Exeunt.

▶ *What plans does Stephano have for the island?*

▶ *Why is Caliban so excited about serving a new master?*

---

40.   **crabs.** Crabapples
41.   **pig-nuts.** Peanuts
42.   **marmozet.** Small monkey from South or Central America
43   **filberts.** Nuts
44.   **Young scamels.** Meaning unknown; possibly shellfish or a type of sea-bird
45.   **trenchering.** Wooden dishes

Responding to the Selection

With your classmates, discuss your reaction to the scene in which Caliban encounters Trinculo and Stephano. Did the scene make you feel sympathy for Caliban, or did you find his behavior to be ridiculous? Did you find this scene to be humorous, or did it sadden you to see how easily the Europeans manipulate Caliban? Does the scene achieve both effects at the same time? Explain.

Reviewing the Selection

Recalling and Interpreting

1. **R:** According to Gonzalo, why should the nobles be happy? In what way do Gonzalo and Adrian perceive the island? In what way do Antonio and Sebastian perceive the island?

2. **I:** Why do you think that Gonzalo and Adrian see the island differently than Antonio and Sebastian do? What does this difference in perception reveal about their characters? Why do Antonio and Sebastian scorn and make fun of Gonzalo?

3. **R:** What does Gonzalo say he would do with the island if he were the king of it? What type of place would the island be? What problem do Antonio and Sebastian point out with Gonzalo's daydream?

4. **I:** What attitude toward a completely "natural" society do you think Shakespeare is expressing in act II, scene i?

5. **R:** What plan does Antonio suggest to Sebastian? What prevents this plan from being carried out?

6. **I:** In what way is the relationship between the two sets of brothers, Prospero and Antonio, and Alonso and Sebastian, similar? To what emotions does Antonio appeal to convince Sebastian to carry out his scheme?

7. **R:** In what way do Trinculo and Stephano perceive Caliban? In what way does Caliban perceive Stephano? What does Caliban decide to do after meeting Stephano and Trinculo? What are Stephano's plans for the island?

8. **I:** What does the way in which Stephano and Trinculo continue to view Caliban reveal about their attitudes toward people of non-European cultures? Compare Caliban's reaction and promises to Stephano to the initial relationship between Caliban and Prospero described in act I. What effect has contact with Europeans had on Caliban?

Synthesizing

9. In act II, characters perceive both the island and each other in vastly different ways. Why do these characters perceive the outside world so differently? What do you think Shakespeare is indicating about perception and reality?

10. What faults in the so-called "civilized" world are pointed out in act II? What adverse effects does Shakespeare reveal that a "civilized" world can have upon a "natural" one? What emotions are stirred in the "civilized" characters when they come into contact with a "natural" world? What flaws does Shakespeare reveal in Caliban, the representative of a "natural" world?

Understanding Literature (QUESTIONS FOR DISCUSSION)

1. **Setting.** The **setting** of a literary work is the time and place in which it occurs, together with all the details used to create a sense of a particular time and place. Many of Shakespeare's dramas feature a place of magical wildness, such as a wood or an island, to which the main characters retreat from the everyday world for a time. In this place, the typical rules for everyday conduct change; characters may take on disguises; the identities or perceptions of characters may change, either permanently or temporarily; and after some confusion or role reversal, a conflict or misunderstanding is resolved. For example, in *A Midsummer Night's Dream,* the relationship between two men and two women is sorted out in a wood outside Athens where fairies dwell and magical transformations occur. What makes the island in *The Tempest* such a setting? In other words, what makes it otherworldly and magical?

2. **Comedy and Conflict.** Originally a literary work with a happy ending, a **comedy** is any lighthearted or humorous work, especially one prepared for the stage or the screen. A **conflict** is a struggle between two forces in a literary work. In Shakespeare's time, *The Tempest* was classified as a comedy, not as a romance. While the first comedies Shakespeare wrote were relatively lighthearted, his later comedies were darker and filled with much more serious conflicts. Often, a tragic ending is narrowly averted in these later comedies. What elements of act II create a comic effect? What conflicts and troubling events undercut the comic effect of act II?

3. **Utopia.** A **utopia** is an imaginary, idealized world. Would you classify as a utopia Gonzalo's vision of how the island would be if he were king? Explain. Would you classify as a utopia the island as it is portrayed in acts I and II? Explain.

Act III

SCENE i: Before Prospero's cell.

Enter FERDINAND, *bearing a log.*

FERDINAND.　There be some sports are painful, and their labor
Delight in them sets off; some kinds of baseness[1]
Are nobly undergone; and most poor matters
Point to rich ends. This my mean task

5　Would be as heavy to me as odious, but
The mistress which I serve quickens[2] what's dead,
And makes my labors pleasures. O, she is
Ten times more gentle than her father's crabbed;
And he's compos'd of harshness. I must remove

10　Some thousands of these logs, and pile them up,
Upon a sore injunction.[3] My sweet mistress
Weeps when she sees me work, and says such baseness
Had never like executor. I forget;
But these sweet thoughts do even refresh my labors,

15　Most busil'est,[4] when I do it.

Enter MIRANDA; *and* PROSPERO [*at a distance, unseen*].

MIRANDA.　　　　　　　Alas, now pray you
Work not so hard. I would the lightning had
Burnt up those logs that you are enjoin'd[5] to pile!
Pray set it down, and rest you. When this burns,
'Twill weep[6] for having wearied you. My father

20　Is hard at study; pray now, rest yourself;
He's safe for these three hours.

FERDINAND.　　　　　　　O most dear mistress,
The sun will set before I shall discharge
What I must strive to do.

MIRANDA.　　　　　If you'll sit down,
I'll bear your logs the while. Pray give me that,

25　I'll carry it to the pile.

◄ *What prevents Ferdinand's task from being odious to him?*

◄ *What task is Prospero making Ferdinand perform?*

◄ *What does Miranda offer to do for Ferdinand?*

ACT III, SCENE i
1. **baseness.** Common, low activity
2. **quickens.** Brings alive
3. **sore injunction.** Stern command
4. **Most busil'est.** Busiest
5. **enjoin'd.** Required
6. **weep.** The heat of the fire will make the log's sap flow

FERDINAND.   No, precious creature,
I had rather crack my sinews,[7] break my back,
Than you should such dishonor undergo,
While I sit lazy by.

MIRANDA.   It would become me
As well as it does you; and I should do it
30   With much more ease, for my good will is to it,
And yours it is against.

PROSPERO. [*Aside.*]   Poor worm, thou art
    infected!
This visitation shows it.

MIRANDA.   You look wearily.

FERDINAND.   No, noble mistress, 'tis fresh morning with
    me
When you are by at night. I do beseech you—
35   Chiefly that I might set it in my prayers—
What is your name?

MIRANDA.   Miranda.—O my father,
I have broke your hest[8] to say so!

FERDINAND.   Admir'd Miranda,
Indeed the top of admiration! worth
What's dearest to the world! Full many a lady
40   I have ey'd with best regard, and many a time
Th' harmony of their tongues hath into bondage
Brought my too diligent ear. For several virtues
Have I lik'd several women, never any
With so full soul but some defect in her
45   Did quarrel with the noblest grace she ow'd[9]
And put it to the foil.[10] But you, O you,
So perfect and so peerless,[11] are created
Of every creature's best!

MIRANDA.   I do not know
One of my sex; no woman's face remember,
50   Save, from my glass, mine own; nor have I seen
More that I may call men than you, good friend,
And my dear father. How features are abroad[12]
I am skilless of; but, by my modesty
(The jewel in my dower),[13] I would not wish

▶ With what is
Miranda "infected"?

▶ What did Miranda
do against her
father's orders?

---

7. **sinews.** Muscles; tendons
8. **hest.** Order
9. **ow'd.** Owned
10. **put . . . foil.** Defeated it
11. **peerless.** Without equal
12. **abroad.** Somewhere else
13. **dower.** Dowry

55   Any companion in the world but you;
     Nor can imagination form a shape,
     Besides yourself, to like of. But I prattle[14]
     Something too wildly, and my father's precepts[15]
     I therein do forget.

     FERDINAND.   I am, in my condition,
60   A prince, Miranda; I do think, a king;
     (I would, not so!), and would no more endure
     This wooden slavery[16] than to suffer
     The flesh-fly blow[17] my mouth. Hear my soul speak:
     The very instant that I saw you, did
65   My heart fly to your service, there resides,
     To make me slave to it, and for your sake
     Am I this patient log-man.

     MIRANDA.   Do you love me?

     FERDINAND.   O heaven, O earth, bear witness to this
         sound,
     And crown what I profess with kind event[18]
70   If I speak true! If hollowly, <u>invert</u>
     What best is boded[19] me to mischief! I,
     Beyond all limit of what else i' th' world,
     Do love, prize, honor you.

     MIRANDA.   I am a fool
     To weep at what I am glad of.

     PROSPERO. [Aside.]   Fair encounter
75   Of two most rare affections! Heavens rain grace
     On that which breeds[20] between 'em!

     FERDINAND.   Wherefore weep you?

     MIRANDA.   At mine unworthiness, that dare not offer
     What I desire to give; and much less take
     What I shall die to want.[21] But this is trifling,

◀ Why does
Ferdinand wish that
he were not a king?
What does this
reveal about his
character?

◀ How does
Prospero really feel
about the relation-
ship between
Ferdinand and
Miranda?

---

14. **prattle.** Chatter
15. **precepts.** Commandments; rules
16. **wooden slavery.** Ordered to be a wood carrier
17. **flesh-fly blow.** Fly to lay its eggs in
18. **kind event.** Pleasing outcome
19. **boded.** Destined
20. **breeds.** Happens
21. **want.** Be deprived of

Words
For
Everyday
Use

in • vert (in vurt´) vt., turn upside down

▶ What does
Miranda say she will
do if Ferdinand does
not want to marry
her?

▶ What have
Miranda and
Ferdinand decided to
do?

▶ What does
Trinculo recognize
about Stephano,
Caliban, and
himself?

80   And all the more it seeks to hide itself,
      The bigger bulk it shows. Hence, bashful cunning,[22]
      And prompt me, plain and holy innocence!
      I am your wife, if you will marry me;
      If not, I'll die your maid. To be your fellow[23]
85   You may deny me, but I'll be your servant,
      Whether you will or no.

      FERDINAND.   My mistress, dearest,
      And I thus humble ever.

      MIRANDA.   My husband, then?

      FERDINAND.   Ay, with a heart as willing
      As bondage e'er[24] of freedom. Here's my hand.

90   MIRANDA.   And mine, with my heart in't. And now
         farewell
      Till half an hour hence.

      FERDINAND.   A thousand thousand![25]
                              Exeunt FERDINAND *and* MIRANDA *severally.*

      PROSPERO.   So glad of this as they I cannot be,
      Who are surpris'd withal;[26] but my rejoicing
      At nothing can be more. I'll to my book,
95   For yet ere supper-time must I perform
      Much business <u>appertaining</u>.   *Exit.*

                SCENE ii: **Another part of the island**

      Enter CALIBAN, STEPHANO, *and* TRINCULO.

      STEPHANO.   Tell not me. When the butt is out,[1] we will
      drink water—not a drop before; therefore bear up and
      board 'em.[2] Servant-monster, drink to me.

      TRINCULO.   Servant-monster? the folly[3] of this island!

---

22. **bashful cunning.** Coyness
23. **fellow.** Mate
24. **e'er.** Ever
25. **a thousand thousand.** A thousand goodbyes
26. **withal.** With it
ACT III, SCENE ii
1. **butt is out.** Wine sack is empty
2. **bear up, and board 'em.** Finish drinking
3. **folly.** Idiocy

Words
For
Everyday
Use

ap • per • tain • ing (ap´ər tān´iŋ) *adj.,* relating to

5   They say there's but five upon this isle: we are three of them; if th' other two be brain'd like us, the state totters.

STEPHANO.   Drink, servant-monster, when I bid thee. Thy eyes are almost set[4] in thy head.

TRINCULO.   Where should they be set else? He were a
10   brave monster indeed if they were set in his tail.

STEPHANO.   My man-monster hath drown'd his tongue in sack. For my part, the sea cannot drown me; I swam, ere I could recover the shore, five and thirty leagues off and on. By this light, thou shalt be my lieutenant,
15   monster, or my standard.[5]

TRINCULO.   Your lieutenant, if you list; he's no standard.[6]

STEPHANO.   We'll not run, Monsieur Monster.

TRINCULO.   Nor go neither; but you'll lie like dogs, and yet say nothing neither.

20   **STEPHANO.**   Moon-calf, speak once in thy life, if thou beest a good moon-calf.

CALIBAN.   How does thy honor? Let me lick thy shoe. I'll not serve him, he is not <u>valiant</u>.

◄ *Whom has Caliban decided he does not admire?*

TRINCULO.   Thou liest,[7] most ignorant monster, I am in
25   case to justle[8] a constable. Why, thou debosh'd[9] fish thou, was there ever man a coward that hath drunk so much sack as I today? Wilt thou tell a monstrous lie, being but half a fish and half a monster?

CALIBAN.   Lo, how he mocks me! Wilt thou let him, my
30   lord?

TRINCULO.   "Lord" quoth he? That a monster should be such a natural![10]

CALIBAN.   Lo, lo, again. Bite him to death, I prithee.

STEPHANO.   Trinculo, keep a good tongue in your head.

---

4. **set.** Sunken (from drinking)
5. **standard.** Upholder of standards
6. **standard.** Someone able to stand
7. **liest.** Lie
8. **justle.** Jostle
9. **debosh'd.** Debauched; corrupt
10. **natural.** Fool

Words For Everyday Use   **val • iant** (val´yənt) *adj.,* brave

► What does
Stephano say
Trinculo must not
do? Why?

35   If you prove a <u>mutineer</u>—the next tree![11] The poor
    monster's my subject, and he shall not suffer indignity.

CALIBAN.   I thank my noble lord. Wilt thou be pleas'd
to harken[12] once again to the suit[13] I made to thee?

STEPHANO.   Marry,[14] will I; kneel, and repeat it. I will
40   stand, and so shall Trinculo.

Enter ARIEL, *invisible.*

CALIBAN.   As I told thee before, I am subject to a tyrant,
A sorcerer, that by his cunning hath
Cheated me of the island.

ARIEL.   Thou liest.

► Who accuses
Caliban of lying?
Who do Stephano
and Caliban believe
is speaking?

CALIBAN.   Thou liest, thou jesting monkey thou!
45   I would my valiant master would destroy thee!
I do not lie.

STEPHANO.   Trinculo, if you trouble him any more in 's
tale, by this hand, I will <u>supplant</u> some of your teeth.

TRINCULO.   Why, I said nothing.

50   **STEPHANO.**   Mum then, and no more.—Proceed.

► What is Caliban's
scheme?

CALIBAN.   I say by sorcery he got this isle;
From me he got it. If thy greatness will
Revenge it on him—for I know thou dar'st,
But this thing dare not—

55   **STEPHANO.**   That's most certain.

CALIBAN.   Thou shalt be lord of it, and I'll serve thee.

STEPHANO.   How now shall this be compass'd? Canst
thou bring me to the party?

CALIBAN.   Yea, yea, my lord. I'll yield him thee asleep,
60   Where thou mayst knock a nail into his head.

ARIEL.   Thou liest; thou canst not.

CALIBAN.   What a pied ninny's[15] this! Thou scurvy patch!
I do beseech thy greatness, give him blows,

---

11. **the next tree.** The next tree will be your hanging place.
12. **harken.** Listen
13. **suit.** Offer
14. **Marry.** Indeed
15. **pied ninny.** Fool or jester in pied, or multicolored clothes

Words For Everyday Use	**mu • ti • neer** (myo͞o t´'n ir´) *n.*, person guilty of revolting against his or her officers (especially on a ship) **sup • plant** (sə plant´) *vt.*, remove by force

And take his bottle from him. When that's gone,
65 He shall drink nought[16] but brine,[17] for I'll not show him
Where the quick freshes[18] are.

STEPHANO. Trinculo, run into no further danger;
interrupt the monster one word further, and, by this
hand, I'll turn my mercy out o' doors, and make a stock-
70 fish[19] of thee.

TRINCULO. Why, what did I? I did nothing. I'll go
farther off.

◄ Why does Stephano beat Trinculo?

STEPHANO. Didst thou not say he lied?

ARIEL. Thou liest.

75 STEPHANO. Do I so? Take thou that. [*Beats* TRINCULO.]
As you like this, give me the lie another time.

TRINCULO. I did not give the lie. Out o' your wits, and
hearing too? A pox o' your bottle! this can sack and
drinking do. A murrain[20] on your monster, and the
80 devil take your fingers!

CALIBAN. Ha, ha, ha!

STEPHANO. Now, forward with your tale.—Prithee stand
further off.

CALIBAN. Beat him enough. After a little time
85 I'll beat him too.

STEPHANO. Stand farther.—Come, proceed.

CALIBAN. Why, as I told thee, 'tis a custom with him
I' th' afternoon to sleep. There thou mayst brain[21] him,
Having first seiz'd his books; or with a log
Batter his skull, or paunch[22] him with a stake,
90 Or cut his wezand[23] with thy knife. Remember
First to possess his books; for without them
He's but a sot,[24] as I am; nor hath not
One spirit to command: they all do hate him
As rootedly as I. Burn but his books.
95 He has brave utensils (for so he calls them)

◄ According to Caliban, what is the source of Prospero's power? According to Caliban, how do the spirits who serve Prospero feel about him?

---

16. **nought.** Nothing
17. **brine.** Salt water
18. **quick freshes.** Fresh water
19. **stock-fish.** Dried fish, so hard it must be beaten to be tenderized
20. **murrain.** Disease
21. **brain.** Hit in the head
22. **paunch.** Stab in the gut
23. **wezand.** Windpipe
24. **sot.** Drunkard

Which when he has a house, he'll deck withal.[25]
And that most deeply to consider is
The beauty of his daughter. He himself
Calls her a nonpareil:[26] I never saw a woman
100 But only Sycorax my dam and she;
But she as far surpasseth Sycorax
As great'st does least.

STEPHANO.   Is it so brave a lass?

CALIBAN.   Ay, lord, she will become[27] thy bed, I warrant.
And bring thee forth brave brood.

105 STEPHANO.   Monster, I will kill this man. His daughter
and I will be king and queen—'save our Graces! and
Trinculo and thyself shall be viceroys.[28] Dost thou like
the plot, Trinculo?

TRINCULO.   Excellent.

110 STEPHANO.   Give me thy hand. I am sorry I beat thee;
but while thou liv'st keep a good tongue in thy head.

CALIBAN.   Within this half hour will he be asleep.
Wilt thou destroy him then?

STEPHANO.   Ay, on mine honor.

ARIEL.   This will I tell my master.

115 CALIBAN.   Thou mak'st me merry; I am full of pleasure,
Let us be jocund:[29] Will you troll the catch[30]
You taught me but while-ere?[31]

STEPHANO.   At thy request, monster, I will do reason,[32]
any reason. Come on, Trinculo, let us sing.   *Sings.*

120   Flout[33] 'em and scout[34] 'em
             And scout 'em and flout 'em
                 Thought is free.

CALIBAN.   That's not the tune.

         ARIEL *plays the tune on a tabor*[35] *and pipe.*

STEPHANO.   What is this same?

125 TRINCULO.   This is the tune of our catch, play'd by the

▶ *What frightens
Stephano and
Trinculo?*

---

25. **deck withal.** Decorate it with
26. **nonpareil.** Without equal
27. **become.** Be right for or suitable to in appearance
28. **viceroys.** Rulers of countries or provinces
29. **jocund.** Jolly
30. **troll the catch.** Sing the round
31. **while-ere.** A little while before
32. **do reason.** Do anything within reason
33. **Flout.** Mock or be scornful of
34. **scout.** Yell at
35. **tabor.** Drum

picture of Nobody.[36]

STEPHANO.   If thou beest a man, show thyself in thy
likeness. If thou beest a devil, take't as thou list.[37]

TRINCULO.   O, forgive me my sins!

130 STEPHANO.   He that dies pays all debts. I defy thee.
Mercy upon us!

CALIBAN.   Art thou afeard?[38]

STEPHANO.   No, monster, not I.

CALIBAN.   Be not afeard, the isle is full of noises,
135 Sounds, and sweet airs, that give delight and hurt not.
Sometimes a thousand twangling instruments
Will hum about mine ears; and sometime voices,
That if I then had wak'd after long sleep,
Will make me sleep again, and then, in dreaming,
140 The clouds methought would open, and show riches
Ready to drop upon me, that when I wak'd
I cried to dream again.

STEPHANO.   This will prove a brave kingdom to me,
where I shall have my music for nothing.

145 CALIBAN.   When Prospero is destroy'd.

STEPHANO.   That shall be by and by. I remember the story.

TRINCULO.   The sound is going away. Let's follow it,
and after do our work.

STEPHANO.   Lead, monster; we'll follow. I would I could
150 see this taborer; he lays it on.

TRINCULO.   Wilt come? I'll follow, Stephano.   *Exeunt.*

SCENE iii: **Another part of the island.**

Enter ALONSO, SEBASTIAN, ANTONIO, GONZALO, ADRIAN,
FRANCISCO, *etc.*

GONZALO.   By'r lakin,[1] I can go no further, sir;
My old bones aches. Here's a maze trod indeed
Through forth-rights and meanders![2] By your patience,
I needs must rest me.

ALONSO.   Old lord, I cannot blame thee,
5 Who am myself attach'd with weariness

◄ *What does
Caliban say about
the island? What
delightful things hap-
pen there?*

---

36. **picture of Nobody.** Traditional representation of a man with head, arms,
and legs but no torso; Trinculo means an invisible being.
37. **list.** Please
38. **afeard.** Afraid
ACT III, SCENE iii
  1. **By'r lakin.** By our Ladykin (the Virgin Mary)
  2. **forth-rights and meanders.** Straight paths and winding ones

To the dulling of my spirits. Sit down, and rest.
Even here I will put off my hope, and keep it
No longer for my flatterer: he is drown'd
Whom thus we stray to find, and the sea mocks
10   Our frustrate search on land. Well, let him go.

▶ *Of what does Antonio remind Sebastian?*

ANTONIO.   [*Aside to* SEBASTIAN.] I am right glad that he's
   so out of hope.
Do not, for one repulse, forego the purpose
That you resolv'd t' effect.

SEBASTIAN.   [*Aside to* ANTONIO.] The next advantage
Will we take throughly.

▶ *What do Antonio and Sebastian plan on doing?*

ANTONIO.   [*Aside to* SEBASTIAN.] Let it be tonight,
15   For, now they are oppress'd with travail, they
Will not, nor cannot, use such vigilance
As when they are fresh.

SEBASTIAN.   [*Aside to* ANTONIO.] I say, tonight. No more.

Solemn and strange music; and PROSPERO *on the top, invisible.*

ALONSO.   What harmony is this? My good friends, hark!

GONZALO.   Marvellous sweet music!

▶ *What do Prospero and his spirits do?*

Enter several strange SHAPES, *bringing in a banquet; and dance about it with gentle actions of salutations; and inviting the King, etc. to eat, they depart.*

20   ALONSO.   Give us kind keepers, heavens! what were
   these?

SEBASTIAN.   A living drollery.[3] Now I will believe
That there are unicorns; that in Arabia
There is one tree, the phoenix' throne, one phoenix
At this hour reigning there.

ANTONIO.   I'll believe both;
25   And what does else want credit, come to me,
And I'll be sworn 'tis true. Travellers ne'er did lie,
Though fools at home condemn 'em.

GONZALO.   If in Naples
I should report this now, would they believe me?
If I should say I saw such islanders
30   (For, certes,[4] these are people of the island)

---

3. **drollery.** Puppet show
4. **certes.** Certain

Who though they are of monstrous shape, yet note
Their manners are more gentle, kind, than of
Our human generation you shall find
Many, nay, almost any.

▶ *What does Gonzalo note about the spirits?*

PROSPERO.　　　[*Aside.*]　Honest lord,
35　Thou hast said well; for some of you there present
Are worse than devils.

◀ *To whom is Prospero referring?*

ALONSO.　　　　　　I cannot too much muse[5]
Such shapes, such gesture, and such sound expressing
(Although they want the use of tongue) a kind
Of excellent dumb[6] discourse.

PROSPERO.　　　　　　[*Aside.*]　Praise in departing.[7]

40　FRANCISCO.　They vanish'd strangely.

SEBASTIAN.　　　　　　　　No matter, since
They have left their viands[8] behind; for we have
stomachs. Will't please you taste of what is here?

ALONSO.　　　　　　Not I.

GONZALO.　Faith, sir, you need not fear. When we were
　　boys,
Who would believe that there were mountaineers,
45　Dew-lapp'd,[9] like bulls, whose throats had hanging at 'em
Wallets of flesh? or that there were such men
Whose heads stood in their breasts?[10] which now we find
Each putter-out of five for one[11] will bring us
Good warrant of.[12]

ALONSO.　　　　I will stand to, and feed,
50　Although my last, no matter, since I feel
The best is past. Brother, my lord the Duke,
Stand to, and do as we.

◀ *Who is about to eat? What does Ariel do? What does Ariel say about the three who were about to dine?*

Thunder and lightning. Enter ARIEL, *like a harpy,*[13] *claps his wings upon the table, and with a quaint device the banquet vanishes.*

ARIEL.　You are three men of sin, whom Destiny,

---

5. **muse.** Ponder
6. **dumb.** Silent
7. **Praise in departing.** Hold your judgment until an event is finished
8. **viands.** Food
9. **Dew-lapp'd.** Loose folds of skin hanging from the throat or chin
10. **heads . . . breasts.** Travelers' tale from medieval times
11. **putter . . . one.** Travelers left a sum of money with their employer to be paid five times over if they returned.
12. **Good warrant of.** Positive declaration
13. **harpy.** Monster with a woman's head and the body of a bird of prey

That hath to instrument[14] this lower world
55 And what is in't, the never-surfeited[15] sea
Hath caus'd to belch up you; and on this island
Where man doth not inhabit—you 'mongst men
Being most unfit to live. I have made you mad;
And even with such-like valor men hang and drown
60 Their proper selves.

ALONSO, SEBASTIAN, *etc. draw their swords.*

You fools! I and my fellows
Are ministers of Fate. The elements,
Of whom your swords are temper'd,[16] may as well
Wound the loud winds, or with bemock'd-at[17] stabs
Kill the still-closing waters, as diminish
65 One dowle[18] that's in my plume.[19] My fellow ministers
Are like invulnerable. If you could hurt,
Your swords are now too massy[20] for your strengths,
And will not be uplifted. But remember
(For that's my business to you) that you three
70 From Milan did supplant good Prospero,
Expos'd unto the sea (which hath requit[21] it)
Him, and his innocent child; for which foul deed
The pow'rs, delaying (not forgetting), have
Incens'd the seas and shores—yea, all the creatures,
75 Against your peace. Thee of thy son, Alonso,
They have bereft;[22] and do pronounce by me
Ling'ring perdition,[23] (worse than any death
Can be at once) shall step by step attend
You and your ways, whose wraths to guard you from—
80 Which here, in this most desolate isle, else falls
Upon your heads—is nothing but heart's sorrow
And a clear life[24] ensuing.

He vanishes in thunder; then, to soft music, enter the SHAPES
*again, and dance, with mocks and mows,[25] and carrying out
the table.*

PROSPERO. Bravely the figure of this harpy hast thou

▶ What does Ariel claim to be?

▶ What explanation does Ariel give the nobles for the tempest? What does Ariel imply about Ferdinand?

▶ What must the three men do to save themselves from the wrath Ariel speaks of?

---

14. **hath to instrument.** Controls
15. **never-surfeited.** Never full or satisfied
16. **temper'd.** Composed; made of
17. **bemock'd-at.** Made fun of
18. **dowle.** Small feather
19. **plume.** Plumage; feathers
20. **massy.** Large
21. **requit.** Avenged for
22. **bereft.** Deprived you
23. **perdition.** Ruin
24. **heart's sorrow . . . clear life.** Repentance and a moral life
25. **mows.** Silly faces

Perform'd, my Ariel; a grace it had, devouring.[26]
85 Of my instruction hast thou nothing bated[27]
In what thou hadst to say; so with good life,
And observation strange,[28] my meaner[29] ministers
Their several kinds have done. My high charms work,
And these mine enemies are all knit up
90 In their distractions.[30] They now are in my pow'r;
And in these fits I leave them, while I visit
Young Ferdinand, whom they suppose is drown'd,
And his and mine lov'd darling.   *Exit above.*

GONZALO.   I' th' name of something holy, sir, why
        stand you
95 In this strange stare?[31]

ALONSO.   O, it is monstrous! monstrous!
Methought the billows[32] spoke, and told me of it;
The winds did sing it to me, and the thunder,
That deep and dreadful organ-pipe, pronounc'd
The name of Prosper; it did base[33] my trespass.
100 Therefore my son i' th' ooze is bedded; and
I'll seek him deeper than e'er plummet[34] sounded,
And with him there lie mudded.[35]   *Exit.*

SEBASTIAN.   But one fiend at a time,
I'll fight their legions o'er.

ANTONIO.   I'll be thy second.
                Exeunt SEBASTIAN *and* ANTONIO.

GONZALO.   All three of them are desperate: their great
        guilt
105 (Like poison given to work a great time after)
Now 'gins to bite the spirits. I do beseech you
(That are of suppler joints) follow them swiftly,
And hinder them from what this ecstasy[36]
May now provoke them to.

ADRIAN.   Follow, I pray you.
                Exeunt omnes.

◄ *In what condition are Alonso, Antonio, and Sebastian?*

◄ *To what does Gonzalo attribute the madness of Alonso, Antonio, and Sebastian?*

---

26. **a grace it had, devouring.** Ariel, as he made the banquet disappear
27. **bated.** Left out
28. **observation strange.** Unusual appearance
29. **meaner.** Lesser
30. **knit . . . distractions.** Caught up in their madness
31. **strange stare.** Strange state
32. **billows.** Waves
33. **base.** Speak in low tones or a deep voice
34. **plummet.** Lead weight hung on a line to determine how deep water is
35. **mudded.** Covered with mud
36. **ecstasy.** Madness

Responding to the Selection

What does the word revenge mean to you? Is vengeance ever justified? Do you think Prospero is taking his revenge too far? Explain.

Reviewing the Selection

Recalling and Interpreting

1. **R:** Why doesn't Ferdinand mind laboring for Prospero? Why does Miranda offer to labor for Ferdinand, both at his present task and in the future as his maid?

2. **I:** Why does Prospero call this scene between Ferdinand and Miranda a "fair encounter of two most rare affections"? Why does Prospero consider the fact that Ferdinand and Miranda are willing to serve each other a sign of true and enduring love?

3. **R:** What plan does Caliban suggest to Stephano?

4. **I:** In what ways is Caliban and Stephano's plan similar to Antonio and Sebastian's plan?

5. **R:** What do Ariel and Prospero cause to appear before Alonso and the nobles? What happens to this apparition when Alonso, Antonio, and Sebastian approach it?

6. **I:** What does Ariel say the apparition, and what becomes of it, reveals about the characters of Alonso, Antonio, and Sebastian? Why might Prospero have decided to reveal the true characters of these men in this way?

7. **R:** What does Ariel say caused the tempest? What does Ariel say about Ferdinand? What happens to Alonso, Antonio, and Sebastian? To what does Gonzalo attribute their strange behavior?

8. **I:** What does Alonso believe has pronounced his guilt? What is his state of mind after Ariel tells him the reason for the tempest and what happened to Ferdinand?

Synthesizing

9. Why do you think Caliban comes up with such a cruel scheme? Is his essential nature ambitious and wicked like Antonio's, or is his behavior a result of the corrupting influence of civilization upon his character? Explain.

10. In classical literature, characters often experienced a tragic downfall for the crime of *hubris,* or excessive pride, when they overstepped the boundary between humanity and the gods. To what extent is Prospero playing God in

act III? Is he guilty of hubris? Why, or why not? Who suffers more, Alonso or Antonio and Sebastian? Whom would you expect Prospero to be most interested in punishing? Is Alonso's punishment at this point in the play fair, or do you think Prospero is going too far in punishing his "inveterate enemy" Alonso?

Understanding Literature (QUESTIONS FOR DISCUSSION)

1. Character and Foil. A **character** is a person (or some-times an animal) who figures in the action of a literary work. A **foil** is a character whose attributes, or characteristics, contrast with and therefore throw into relief the attributes of another character. In many ways, Miranda and Caliban are similar: they were both raised by a solitary magician parent, Prospero educated Miranda who in turn educated Caliban with her father's help, both have lived far from civilization and have seen few people, and both believe that nobles are gods when they first see them. Why then might Miranda and Caliban be considered each other's foils? In what way do their similar backgrounds highlight their differences?

2. Parallelism. **Parallelism** is a rhetorical technique in which a writer emphasizes the equal value or weight of two or more ideas by expressing them in the same grammatical form. Parallelism may also be used as an organizational technique in longer literary works. In *The Tempest,* Antonio and Sebastian's plot to acquire kingship of Naples by killing Alonso as he sleeps parallels Caliban and Stephano's plan to acquire kingship of the island by killing Prospero as he sleeps. These plots also parallel the background of the play, when Antonio and Alonso schemed to deprive Prospero of his dukedom. Why do you think Shakespeare creates three parallel plots in which characters strive to gain political power? What do these plots reveal about the "civilized" world? about the "natural" world? In what way do the plots or the persons doing the scheming differ? In what way do their similarities comment upon such schemes in general?

3. Iambic Pentameter and Prose. An **iamb** is a poetic foot (or unit of rhythm) containing one weakly stressed syl-lable followed by one strongly stressed syllable. **Pentameter** is a term for a five-foot line. **Prose** is the broad term used to describe all writing that is not poetry. As a general rule, Shakespeare usually wrote lines for his characters of noble background or high status in iambic pentameter, with some occasional variation from this verse form, while he wrote the lines of characters of lower status in prose. The effect is that the characters of high status speak in beautiful, highly elevated language, while the characters of lower status speak in the more common language of everyday life. In this play, Caliban often speaks in prose, but he also speaks in verse. Analyze Caliban's speech: "Be not afeard; the isle is full of noises," in act III, scene ii to determine its meter. In what way would you characterize the language in this speech—is it poetic or is it the language of everyday speech? What does the fact that Shakespeare chose to have Caliban speak in verse such as this reveal about Caliban's character?

4. Stage Directions, Spectacle, and Allegory. Stage directions are notes included in a play for the purpose of describing how something should be performed on stage. In drama, the **spectacle** is all the elements that are presented to the senses of the audience, including the lights, setting, costumes, makeup, music, sound effects, and movements of the actors. An **allegory** is a work in which each element symbolizes, or represents, something else. Shakespeare included more stage directions in *The Tempest* than in many of his plays. Why are stage directions particularly crucial in act III, scene iii? Would you be able to gain an understanding of the scene from the dialogue alone? What extraordinary elements of spectacle are used in the banquet incident in act III, scene iii? In the sixteenth and seventeenth centuries, masques were popular among courtiers. These were brief allegorical dramas that were lavish in spectacle and were performed by masked actors. In what way is the banquet incident similar to a court masque? If the banquet is an element of an allegory, what does its appearance and disappearance represent?

Act IV

SCENE i: Before Prospero's cell.

Enter PROSPERO, FERDINAND, *and* MIRANDA.

PROSPERO.   If I have too <u>austerely</u> punish'd you,
Your compensation makes amends, for I
Have given you here a third of mine own life,
Or that for which I live; who once again
5   I tender to thy hand.[1] All thy vexations[2]
Were but my trials of thy love, and thou
Hast strangely stood the test. Here, afore Heaven,
I <u>ratify</u> this my rich gift. O Ferdinand,
Do not smile at me that I boast her off,[3]
10   For thou shalt find she will outstrip all praise
And make it halt behind her.

FERDINAND.   I do believe it
Against an oracle.

PROSPERO.   Then, as my gift, and thine own acquisition
Worthily purchas'd, take my daughter. But
15   If thou dost break her virgin-knot before
All sanctimonious[4] ceremonies may
With full and holy rite be minist'red,
No sweet <u>aspersion</u> shall the heavens let fall
To make this contract grow: but barren hate,
20   Sour-ey'd disdain, and discord shall bestrew[5]
The union of your bed with weeds so loathly[6]
That you shall hate it both. Therefore take heed,
As Hymen's[7] lamps shall light you.

FERDINAND.   As I hope
For quiet days, fair issue,[8] and long life,
25   With such love as 'tis now, the murkiest den,

◄ What "compensation" is Prospero giving Ferdinand for having punished him?

---

1. **tender to thy hand.** Give to you
2. **vexations.** Troubles
3. **boast her off.** Speak highly of her
4. **sanctimonious.** Sacred, holy
5. **bestrew.** Scatter; marriage beds were traditionally strewn with flowers.
6. **loathly.** Hateful; awful
7. **Hymen's lamps.** Hymen, Greek god of marriage, whose torch burned with a clear flame if a marriage was favorable
8. **fair issue.** Beautiful children

Words For Everyday Use

aus • tere • ly (ôs stir′lē) *adv.*, harshly
rat • i • fy (rat′ə fī´) *vt.*, confirm
as • per • sion (ə spʉr′zhən) *n.*, sprinkling of water, as in baptism

The most opportune place, the strong'st suggestion
Our worser genius can,[9] shall never melt
Mine honor into lust, to take away
The edge of that day's celebration,
30 When I shall think, or Phoebus' steeds [10] are founder'd,[11]
Or Night kept chain'd below.

PROSPERO.   Fairly spoke.
Sit then and talk with her; she is thine own.
What, Ariel! My industrious servant, Ariel!

Enter ARIEL.

ARIEL.   What would my potent master? [12] here I am.

35 PROSPERO.   Thou and thy meaner fellows your last
    service
Did worthily perform; and I must use you
In such another trick. Go bring the rabble,[13]
(O'er whom I give thee pow'r) here to this place.
Incite them to quick motion, for I must
40 Bestow upon the eyes of this young couple
Some vanity [14] of mine art. It is my promise,
And they expect it from me.

ARIEL.   Presently?

PROSPERO.   Ay, with a twink.[15]

ARIEL.   Before you can say "come" and "go,"
45   And breathe twice and cry "so, so,"
          Each one, tripping on his toe,
          Will be here with mop and mow.
          Do you love me, master? no?

PROSPERO.   Dearly, my delicate Ariel. Do not approach
50 Till thou dost hear me call.

ARIEL.   Well; I conceive.[16]   *Exit.*

---

9. **Our worser genius can.** My bad angel is capable of
10. **Phoebus' steeds.** Greek sun god's horses
11. **founder'd.** Become lame
12. **What would . . . master?** What do you ask of me?
13. **rabble.** Group of lesser spirits
14. **vanity.** Show
15. **twink.** Quickly
16. **conceive.** Think

► What has Prospero promised the couple?

Words
For
Everyday
Use   **in • cite** (in sīt') *vt.,* set into motion, urge

PROSPERO.   Look thou be true; do not give dalliance[17]
Too much the rein. The strongest oaths are straw[18]
To th' fire i' th' blood. Be more abstemious,[19]
Or else, good night your vow!

FERDINAND.   I warrant you, sir;
55   The white cold virgin snow upon my heart
Abates the ardor of my liver.[20]

PROSPERO.   Well.
Now come, my Ariel, bring a corollary,[21]
Rather than want[22] a spirit. Appear, and pertly!
No tongue! all eyes! Be silent.   *Soft music.*

Enter IRIS.[23]

60   **IRIS.**   Ceres,[24] most bounteous lady, thy rich leas
Of wheat, rye, barley, vetches, oats, and pease;[25]
Thy turfy mountains, where live nibbling sheep,
And flat meads thatch'd with stover,[26] them to keep;
Thy banks with pioned and twilled[27] brims,
65   Which spungy[28] April at thy hest[29] betrims,
To make cold nymphs chaste crowns; and thy broom-
          groves,
Whose shadow the dismissed bachelor loves,
Being lass-lorn;[30] thy pole-clipt[31] vineyard,
And thy sea-marge,[32] sterile and rocky-hard,
70   Where thou thyself dost air—the Queen o' the sky,[33]
Whose wat'ry arch and messenger am I,
Bids thee leave these, and with her sovereign Grace,
Here on this grass-plot, in this very place,
To come and sport. Her peacocks[34] fly amain.[35]

◄ *Of what is Ceres goddess?*

---

17. **dalliance.** Flirtation
18. **straw.** Weak
19. **abstemious.** Moderate
20. **abates the ardor . . . liver.** Lessens the strength of my passion
21. **corollary.** Extra
22. **want.** Lack
23. **Iris.** Greek goddess of the rainbow
24. **Ceres.** Roman goddess of agriculture
25. **leas . . . vetches . . . pease.** Leas—pastures; *vetches*—types of plants used for fodder, or cattle feed; *pease*—peas
26. **stover.** Hay used as winter feed
27. **pioned and twilled.** Cut out by a stream and held by intertwined branches
28. **spungy.** Wet
29. **hest.** Order, command
30. **lass-lorn.** Distraught over a lost love
31. **pole-clipt.** Pruned, clipped back
32. **sea-marge.** Seashore
33. **Queen o' the sky.** Juno, Roman goddess of the heavens
34. **peacocks.** Peacocks were the birds of Juno.
35. **amain.** Swiftly

75   Approach, rich Ceres, her to entertain.

Enter CERES.

▶ *Of what is Iris goddess?*

CERES.   Hail, many-colored messenger, that ne'er
Dost disobey the wife of Jupiter;[36]
Who with thy saffron[37] wings upon my flow'rs
Diffusest[38] honey-drops, refreshing show'rs,

80   And with each end of thy blue bow dost crown
My bosky[39] acres and my unshrubb'd down,
Rich scarf to my proud earth—why hath thy Queen
Summon'd me hither, to this short-grass'd green?

▶ *Why has Ceres been called to the island?*

IRIS.   A contract of true love to celebrate,

85   And some donation freely to estate [40]
On the bless'd lovers.

▶ *Of which gods do Iris and Ceres disapprove? Why?*

CERES.   Tell me, heavenly bow,
If Venus or her son,[41] as thou dost know,
Do now attend the Queen? Since they did plot
The means that dusky Dis[42] my daughter got,

90   Her and her blind boy's scandall'd company
I have forsworn.

IRIS.   Of her society
Be not afraid. I met her Deity
Cutting the clouds towards Paphos;[43] and her son
Dove-drawn[44] with her. Here thought they to have done

95   Some wanton[45] charm upon this man and maid,
Whose vows are, that no bed-right shall be paid
Till Hymen's torch be lighted; but in vain,
Mars's[46] hot minion[47] is return'd again;
Her waspish-headed[48] son has broke his arrows,

100   Swears he will shoot no more, but play with sparrows,
And be a boy right out.

JUNO *alights.*

---

36. **Jupiter.** Roman god of the heavens; his wife is Juno
37. **saffron.** Rich yellow color
38. **Diffusest.** Diffuse, scatter
39. **bosky.** Forested
40. **estate.** Give
41. **son.** Cupid
42. **Dis.** Pluto, Roman god of the underworld who stole Ceres's daughter, Proserpine, to be his queen
43. **Paphos.** City in Cyprus and the center of Venus's worship
44. **Dove-drawn.** The chariot of Venus was drawn by sacred doves.
45. **wanton.** Reckless
46. **Mars's.** Of the Roman god of war
47. **minion.** Mistress (Venus, lover of Mars)
48. **waspish-headed.** Spoiled; grouchy

CERES.   Highest Queen of state,
Great Juno, comes, I know her by her <u>gait</u>.

JUNO.   How does my <u>bounteous</u> sister? Go with me
To bless this twain,[49] that they may prosperous be,
105 And honor'd in their issue.   *They sing.*

JUNO.   Honor, riches, marriage-blessing,
                Long continuance, and increasing,
                Hourly joys be still upon you!
                Juno sings her blessings on you.

110 CERES.   Earth's increase, foison[50] plenty,
                Barns and <u>garners</u> never empty;
                Vines with clust'ring bunches growing,
                Plants with goodly burthen bowing;
                Spring come to you at the farthest
115   In the very end of harvest!
                Scarcity and want shall shun you,
                Ceres' blessing so is on you.

FERDINAND.   This is a most majestic vision, and
Harmonious charmingly. May I be bold,
120 To think these spirits?

PROSPERO.   Spirits, which by mine art
I have from their confines call'd to enact
My present fancies.

FERDINAND.   Let me live here ever;
So rare a wond'red father and a wise
Makes this place Paradise.

         JUNO *and* CERES *whisper, and send* IRIS *on employment.*

PROSPERO.   Sweet now, silence!
125 Juno and Ceres whisper seriously;
There's something else to do. Hush and be mute,
Or else our spell is marr'd.[51]

IRIS.   You nymphs, call'd Naiades, of the windring[52]
         brooks,
With your sedg'd[53] crowns and ever-harmless looks,

◄ *What blessing does Juno give to Miranda and Ferdinand?*

◄ *What blessing does Ceres give to Miranda and Ferdinand?*

---

49. **twain.** Two; pair
50. **foison.** Abundance
51. **marr'd.** Marred; spoiled
52. **windring.** Winding
53. **sedg'd.** Grassy

Words For Everyday Use

gait (gāt) *n.,* manner of moving on foot
boun • te • ous (boun'tē əs) *adj.,* giving freely and generously without restraint
gar • ner (gär'nər) *n.,* place for storing

130 Leave your crisp channels, and on this green land
Answer your summons; Juno does command.
Come, temperate nymphs, and help to celebrate
A contract of true love; be not too late.

Enter certain NYMPHS.

You sunburn'd sicklemen, of August weary,
135 Come hither from the furrow[54] and be merry.
Make holiday; your rye-straw hats put on,
And these fresh nymphs encounter every one
In country footing.

Enter certain REAPERS, *properly habited: they join with the*
NYMPHS *in a graceful dance, towards the end whereof*
PROSPERO *starts suddenly, and speaks; after which, to a*
strange, hollow, and confused noise, they heavily vanish.

▶ Who interrupts
the dance? What
does Prospero sud-
denly remember?

PROSPERO.   [*Aside.*] I had forgot that foul conspiracy
140 Of the beast Caliban and his confederates
Against my life. The minute of their plot
Is almost come. [*To the* SPIRITS.] Well done, avoid; no
more!

FERDINAND.   This is strange. Your father's in some
passion
That works him strongly.

MIRANDA.   Never till this day
145 Saw I him touch'd with anger, so distemper'd.

PROSPERO.   You do look, my son, in a mov'd sort,
As if you were dismay'd; be cheerful, sir.
Our <u>revels</u> now are ended. These our actors

▶ What is Prospero
saying about the
world? What is he
saying about people?
What might he be
saying about actors
and acting?

(As I foretold you) were all spirits, and
150 Are melted into air, into thin air,
And, like the baseless fabric of this vision,
The cloud-capp'd tow'rs, the gorgeous palaces,
The solemn temples, the great globe itself,
Yea, all which it inherit, shall dissolve,
155 And like this insubstantial pageant faded
Leave not a rack[55] behind. We are such stuff

---

54. **furrow.** Narrow groove made in the ground for planting seeds
55. **rack.** Cloud

Words
For
Everyday
Use

rev • el (rev´əl) *n.,* festive merrymaking

As dreams are made on; and our little life
Is rounded with a sleep. Sir, I am vex'd;
Bear with my weakness, my old brain is troubled.
160   Be not disturb'd with my <u>infirmity</u>.
If you be pleas'd, retire into my cell,
And there <u>repose</u>. A turn or two I'll walk
To still my beating mind.

FERDINAND AND MIRANDA.   We wish your peace.

165   PROSPERO.   [*To* ARIEL.] Come with a thought. [*To*
      FERDINAND *and* MIRANDA.] I thank thee.
                          [*Exeunt.*] Ariel! come.
Enter ARIEL.

ARIEL.   Thy thoughts I cleave[56] to. What's thy pleasure?

PROSPERO.   Spirit,
We must prepare to meet with Caliban.

ARIEL.   Ay, my commander. When I presented Ceres,
I thought to have told thee of it, but I fear'd
170   Lest I might anger thee.

PROSPERO.   Say again, where didst thou leave these
      varlots?[57]

ARIEL.   I told you, sir, they were red-hot with drinking,
So full of valor that they smote[58] the air
For breathing in their faces; beat the ground
175   For kissing of their feet; yet always bending
Towards their project. Then I beat my tabor,
At which, like unback'd[59] colts they prick'd their ears,
Advanced[60] their eyelids, lifted up their noses
As they smelt music. So I charm'd their ears
180   That calf-like they my lowing follow'd through
Tooth'd <u>briers</u>, sharp furzes, pricking goss, and thorns,
Which ent'red their frail shins. At last I left them
I' th' filthy-mantled[61] pool beyond your cell,

◄ What does Prospero say is wrong?

◄ What did Ariel find Caliban, Stephano, and Trinculo doing? What did Ariel do to them?

◄ Where did Ariel leave Caliban, Stephano, and Trinculo?

---

56. **cleave.** Cling
57. **varlots.** Scoundrels
58. **smote.** Hit or strike hard
59. **unback'd.** Untrained, unridden
60. **Advanced.** Opened
61. **filthy-mantled.** Covered with scum

Words For Everyday Use

in • fir • mi • ty (in fʉr′mə tē) *n.*, feebleness, weakness
re • pose (ri pōz′) *vt.*, lie at rest
bri • er (brī′ər) *n.*, any prickly or thorny bush

There dancing up to th' chins, that the foul lake
185 O'erstunk their feet.

PROSPERO.   This was well done, my bird.
Thy shape invisible retain thou still.
The trumpery[62] in my house, go bring it hither,
For stale[63] to catch these thieves.

ARIEL.   I go, I go.   *Exit.*

► *How does
Prospero feel about
Caliban's scheme? To
what does he
attribute this
scheme?*

PROSPERO.   A devil, a born devil, on whose nature
190 Nurture can never stick; on whom my pains,
Humanely taken, all, all lost, quite lost;
And as with age his body uglier grows,
So his mind cankers.[64] I will plague them all,
Even to roaring.

Enter ARIEL, *loaden with glistering apparel, etc.*

Come, hang them on this line.[65]

PROSPERO *and* ARIEL *remain, invisible. Enter* CALIBAN,
STEPHANO, *and* TRINCULO, *all wet.*

195 CALIBAN.   Pray you tread softly, that the blind mole
    may not
Hear a foot fall: we now are near his cell.

STEPHANO.   Monster, your fairy, which you say is a
harmless fairy, has done little better than play'd the
Jack[66] with us.

200 TRINCULO.   Monster, I do smell all horse-piss, at which
my nose is in great <u>indignation</u>.

STEPHANO.   So is mine. Do you hear, monster? If I
should take a displeasure against you, look you—

TRINCULO.   Thou wert but a lost monster.

205 CALIBAN.   Good my lord, give me thy favor still.
Be patient, for the prize I'll bring thee to
Shall hoodwink[67] this mischance; therefore speak softly,

---

62. **trumpery.** Showy things
63. **stale.** Bait
64. **cankers.** Becomes filled with hatred
65. **line.** Lime tree
66. **Jack.** Trickster
67. **hoodwink.** Cheat or trick

Words
For
Everyday
Use
in • dig • na • tion (in´dig nā´ shən) *n.,* anger or scorn

All's hush'd as midnight yet.

TRINCULO. Ay, but to lose our bottles in the pool—

210 STEPHANO. There is not only disgrace and dishonor in that, monster, but an infinite loss.

TRINCULO. That's more to me than my wetting; yet this is your harmless fairy, monster!

STEPHANO. I will fetch off my bottle, though I be o'er
215 ears[68] for my labor.

CALIBAN. Prithee, my king, be quiet. Seest thou here,
This is the mouth o' the cell. No noise, and enter.
Do that good mischief which may make this island
Thine own for ever, and I, thy Caliban,
220 For aye thy foot-licker.

STEPHANO. Give me thy hand. I do begin to have bloody thoughts.

◄ What interrupts the conspirators just when Stephano begins to have "bloody thoughts"?

TRINCULO. O King Stephano! O peer! O worthy Stephano! look what a wardrobe here is for thee!

225 CALIBAN. Let it alone, thou fool, it is but trash.

TRINCULO. O, ho, monster! We know what belongs to a frippery.[69] O King Stephano!

STEPHANO. Put off that gown, Trinculo. By this hand, I'll have that gown.

230 TRINCULO. Thy Grace shall have it.

CALIBAN. The dropsy drown[70] this fool! what do you mean
To dote thus on such luggage? Let't alone
And do the murder first. If he awake,
From toe to crown he'll fill our skins with pinches,
235 Make us strange stuff.

◄ What does Caliban urge Stephano and Trinculo to do? Of what does he warn his fellow conspirators?

STEPHANO. Be you quiet, monster. Mistress line, is not this my jerkin? Now is the jerkin under the line. Now, jerkin, you are like to lose your hair, and prove a bald jerkin.[71]

240 TRINCULO. Do, do; we steal by line and level,[72] and't like your Grace.

---

68. **o'er ears.** Over my ears in water
69. **frippery.** Used clothing shop
70. **dropsy drown.** (May a) swelling disease suffocate
71. **Now is the jerkin . . . a bald jerkin.** *Jerkin*—leather jacket; Stephano is making reference to the popular belief that sailors on voyages "under the line," or south of the equator, lost their hair.
72. **we steal by line and level.** We steal professionally and with skill, as a builder uses a plumb-line and carpenter's level.

STEPHANO. I thank thee for that jest; here's a garment for't. Wit shall not go unrewarded while I am king of this country. "Steal by line and level" is an excellent
245   pass of pate;[73] there's another garment for't.

TRINCULO. Monster, come put some lime[74] upon your fingers, and away with the rest.

▶ What does Caliban fear will happen?

CALIBAN. I will have none on't. We shall lose our time, And all be turn'd to barnacles,[75] or to apes
250   With foreheads villanous low.

STEPHANO. Monster, lay-to your fingers. Help to bear this away where my hogshead of wine is, or I'll turn you out of my kingdom. Go to, carry this.

TRINCULO. And this.

255 **STEPHANO.** Ay, and this.

A noise of hunters heard. Enter divers SPIRITS, *in shape of dogs and hounds, hunting them about;* PROSPERO *and* ARIEL *setting them on.*

PROSPERO. Hey, Mountain, hey!

ARIEL. Silver! there it goes, Silver!

PROSPERO. Fury, Fury! there, Tyrant, there! hark, hark!

                     CALIBAN, STEPHANO, *and* TRINCULO *are driven out.*

▶ What punishment does Prospero order upon Caliban, Stephano, and Trinculo?

Go charge my goblins that they grind their joints
260   With dry convulsions, shorten up their <u>sinews</u>
With aged cramps, and more pinch-spotted make them
Than pard[76] or cat o' mountain.

ARIEL.   Hark, they roar!

▶ What does Prospero say about this hour?

PROSPERO. Let them be hunted soundly. At this hour
265   Lie at my mercy all mine enemies.
Shortly shall all my labors end, and thou
Shalt have the air at freedom. For a little
Follow, and do me service.

                                 Exeunt.

---

73. **pass of pate.** Show of clever thinking
74. **lime.** Sticky substance, jokingly said to coat thieves' hands
75. **barnacles.** "Barnacle geese," wild geese supposed to grow from shellfish
76. **pard.** Leopard

Words For Everyday Use   **sin • ew** (sin'yo͞o) *n.,* tendon; source of power or strength

Responding to the Selection

In small groups, discuss whether or not you would like to have a father like Prospero. What would the advantages and disadvantages be? What do you think Prospero's attitude would be toward a child who disobeyed his wishes?

Reviewing the Selection

Recalling and Interpreting

1. **R:** What does Prospero tell Ferdinand he must not do before marriage? What does Prospero say will happen if Ferdinand does not follow his advice? What does Ferdinand say about Prospero's advice?

2. **I:** What may Prospero worry will happen to his plans to regain political power if Ferdinand and Miranda do not follow his advice? What qualities or characteristics does Prospero seem to value? Does Ferdinand possess these characteristics? Explain. Why might Miranda remain silent throughout her father's and Ferdinand's conversation, as well as through most of act IV?

3. **R:** What goddesses appear in the masque, or show, that Prospero presents, and what blessings do they give Ferdinand and Miranda? What gods does Iris say have been frustrated in their schemes? What were these gods trying to do? Who else does Prospero cause to appear?

4. **I:** What is Prospero's motivation for showing this scene to Ferdinand and Miranda? What vision of marriage does Prospero present in this scene?

5. **R:** What does Prospero suddenly remember? What does Miranda say about her father? What does Prospero say about Caliban's nature? What does he plan to do to the conspirators?

6. **I:** Why is Prospero especially angry with Caliban? Is his anger justified? Of what similar experience might Caliban's plot remind him?

7. **R:** What does Prospero instruct Ariel to do to foil the conspirators' plot? Which characters are fooled by this trick? Which character is not fooled by this trick?

8. **I:** What does Caliban's reaction to Prospero's trick reveal about his character? What do Stephano's and Trinculo's reactions reveal about their characters?

Synthesizing

9. You have already read about court masques in act III. In what way is the masque in act IV similar to the masque in act III? In what way is it different? Compare and contrast Prospero's motivation for presenting each of these masques. Why does Prospero break off the masque in act III? Why does he break off the masque in act IV?

10. Prospero's speech in act IV, scene i, beginning "These our actors . . . were all spirits" is sometimes regarded as Shakespeare's farewell to the theater. Look closely at the speech. The term *globe* might refer to Shakespeare's Globe Theater as well as to the world, and when Prospero says "We are such stuff as dreams are made on," he might be referring to actors or even to playwrights. In what ways is Prospero like a playwright? Do you think Shakespeare intended this passage as his farewell to the theater, or did he intend something entirely different? Could the passage be read as a farewell to life itself? If so, what philosophy does the speech present? Explain and support your reasoning with evidence from the text.

Understanding Literature (QUESTIONS FOR DISCUSSION)

1. **Simile, Metaphor, and Tone.** A **simile** is a comparison using *like* or *as*. A **metaphor** is a figure of speech in which one thing is spoken or written about as if it were another. **Tone** is the emotional attitude toward the reader or toward the subject implied by a literary work. Prospero's speech in act IV, scene i, beginning "These our actors . . . were all spirits" is prefaced by an attempt to reassure Ferdinand and to tell him not to be "dismay'd" but "cheerful." Nevertheless, Prospero quickly digresses from this purpose to meditate on far less reassuring subjects. To what does Prospero compare "The cloud-capp'd tow'rs, the gorgeous palaces, / The solemn temples, the great globe itself"? What metaphor does Prospero use to describe "We" and "life"? What tone is expressed through the use of this simile and this metaphor? What tone is expressed in the lines "Bear with my weakness; my old brain is troubled; / Be not disturb'd with my infirmity" and following?

2. Dramatic Irony and Aside. **Dramatic irony** is a difference between appearance and reality in which something is known by the reader or audience but unknown to the characters. An **aside** is a statement made by a character in a play, intended to be heard by the audience but not by the other characters on the stage. When Prospero makes his aside immediately following the dispelling of the court masque, what does the audience learn that the other characters in the play do not know? When Prospero and Ariel watch Stephano and Trinculo stopping to collect the rich garments and Caliban pleading with them to hurry, Prospero and Ariel are visible to the audience but invisible to Caliban, Stephano, and Trinculo. In what way is the use of characters that are visible to the audience but invisible to other characters similar to an aside? Why might the scene in which Caliban pleads with Stephano and Trinculo to hurry up and warns them that if Prospero wakes they will be severely punished be considered an example of dramatic irony?

Act V

SCENE i: Before Prospero's cell.

Enter PROSPERO *in his magic robes, and* ARIEL.

PROSPERO.   Now does my project gather to a head:
My charms crack not; my spirits obey; and Time
Goes upright with his carriage.[1] How's the day?

ARIEL.   On the sixt hour, at which time, my lord,
5 You said our work should cease.

PROSPERO.   I did say so,
When first I raised the tempest. Say, my spirit,
How fares the king and 's followers?

ARIEL.   Confin'd together
In the same fashion as you gave in charge,
Just as you left them; all prisoners, sir,
10 In the line-grove which weather-fends[2] your cell;
They cannot boudge till your release. The King,
His brother, and yours, abide all three distracted,
And the remainder mourning over them,
Brimful of sorrow and dismay; but chiefly
15 Him that you term'd,[3] sir, "the good old Lord Gonzalo,"
His tears run down his beard like winter's drops
From eaves of reeds.[4] Your charm so strongly works 'em
That if you now beheld them, your affections
Would become tender.

PROSPERO.   Dost thou think so, spirit?

20 ARIEL.   Mine would, sir, were I human.

PROSPERO.   And mine shall.
Hast thou, which art but air, a touch, a feeling
Of their afflictions, and shall not myself,
One of their kind, that relish[5] all as sharply
Passion as they, be kindlier mov'd than thou art?
25 Though with their high wrongs I am stroock to th' quick,
Yet with my nobler reason, 'gainst my fury

---

1. **Goes upright with his carriage.** Walks upright because his load has been lessened by previous events
2. **weather-fends.** Acts as a wind barrier
3. **term'd.** Called; named
4. **winter's drops / From eaves of reeds.** Icicles hanging from the eaves of a thatched roof
5. **relish.** Experience

▶ What time is it? What is significant about this time?

▶ Where are the nobles? In what condition are the king, his brother, and Prospero's brother? How do the other nobles feel about Alonso, Antonio, and Sebastian's condition?

▶ What does Ariel say would happen if Prospero saw his prisoners?

▶ What does Prospero say will happen?

Do I take part. The rarer action is
In virtue than in vengeance. They being <u>penitent</u>,
The sole drift of my purpose doth extend
30 Not a frown further. Go release them, Ariel.
My charms I'll break, their senses I'll restore,
And they shall be themselves.

ARIEL.   I'll fetch them, sir.   *Exit.*
PROSPERO *traces a magic circle with his staff.*

PROSPERO.   Ye elves of hills, brooks, standing lakes, and
        groves,
And ye that on the sands with printless foot
35 Do chase the ebbing Neptune,[6] and do fly him
When he comes back; you demi-puppets[7] that
By moonshine do the green sour ringlets make,[8]
Whereof the ewe[9] not bites; and you whose pastime
Is to make midnight mushrumps,[10] that rejoice
40 To hear the solemn curfew: by whose aid,
(Weak masters though ye be) I have bedimm'd[11]
The noontide sun, call'd forth the mutinous winds,
And 'twixt the green sea and the azur'd[12] vault
Set roaring war; to the dread rattling thunder
45 Have I given fire, and rifted[13] Jove's stout oak
With his own bolt; the strong-based promontory[14]
Have I made shake, and by the spurs pluck'd up
The pine and cedar. Graves at my command
Have wak'd their sleepers, op'd,[15] and let 'em forth
50 By my so potent art. But this rough magic
I here abjure,[16] and, when I have requir'd
Some heavenly music (which even now I do)
To work mine end upon their senses that
This airy charm is for, I'll break my staff,

◄ *What does Prospero say about vengeance? What does Prospero seek from Alonso, Antonio, and Sebastian? What is Prospero going to do with the prisoners?*

◄ *What has Prospero used his art to accomplish?*

◄ *What does Prospero say he will do with his art, or his "rough magic"? What will he do with the objects that give him power?*

---

6. **Neptune.** Roman god of the sea
7. **demi-puppets.** Elves and fairies
8. **green sour ringlets.** "Fairy rings" in the grass
9. **ewe.** Female sheep
10. **mushrumps.** Mushrooms
11. **bedimm'd.** Lessened the light of
12. **azur'd vault.** Bright blue-colored sky
13. **rifted.** Split
14. **promontory.** Peak of a high land that juts out over a body of water
15. **oped.** Opened
16. **abjure.** Give up

Words
For
Everyday
Use

pen • i • tent (pen'i tənt) *adj.,* truly sorry for having sinned and willing to atone

55 Bury it certain fathoms in the earth,
And deeper than did ever plummet sound
I'll drown my book.   *Solemn music.*

Here enters ARIEL *before; then* ALONSO, *with a frantic gesture,*
attended by GONZALO; SEBASTIAN *and* ANTONIO *in like*
manner, attended by ADRIAN *and* FRANCISCO. *They all*
enter the circle which PROSPERO *had made, and there*
stand charm'd; which PROSPERO *observing, speaks.*

A solemn air, and the best comforter
To an unsettled fancy, cure thy brains,
60 Now useless, boil'd within thy skull! There stand,
For you are spell-stopp'd.
Holy Gonzalo, honorable man,
Mine eyes, ev'n sociable to the show of thine,
Fall fellowly drops.[17] The charm dissolves apace,[18]
65 And as the morning steals upon the night,
Melting the darkness, so their rising senses
Begin to chase the ignorant fumes[19] that mantle
Their clearer reason. O good Gonzalo,
My true preserver, and a loyal sir
70 To him you follow'st! I will pay thy graces
Home both in word and deed. Most cruelly
Didst thou, Alonso, use me and my daughter;
Thy brother was a furtherer[20] in the act.
Thou art pinch'd for't[21] now, Sebastian. Flesh and blood,
75 You, brother mine, that entertain'd ambition,
Expell'd remorse and nature, whom, with Sebastian
(Whose inward pinches therefore are most strong),
Would here have kill'd your king, I do forgive thee,
Unnatural though thou art.—Their understanding
80 Begins to swell, and the approaching tide
Will shortly fill the reasonable shores
That now lie foul and muddy. Not one of them
That yet looks on me, or would know me! Ariel,
Fetch me the hat and rapier[22] in my cell.

Exit ARIEL, *and returns immediately.*

85 I will discase[23] me, and myself present
As I was sometime Milan. Quickly, spirit,
Thou shalt ere long be free.

ARIEL *sings and helps to attire him.*

---

17. **Fall fellowly drops.** Let fall tears of sympathy
18. **apace.** Swiftly
19. **ignorant fumes.** Fumes that impair understanding
20. **furtherer.** Helper; aid
21. **Thou art pinch'd for't now.** You are in trouble now.
22. **rapier.** Sword
23. **discase.** Disrobe of magician's clothing

► What does Prospero do to Alonso, Antonio, and Sebastian?

► What promise does Prospero make to Gonzalo?

► For what does Prospero reproach Alonso?

► What does Prospero say about his brother? What does Prospero say he offers him?

► How does Prospero wish to appear before Alonso, Antonio, and Sebastian?

ARIEL. Where the bee sucks, there suck I,
In a cowslip's bell I lie;
90 There I couch[24] when owls do cry.
On the bat's back I do fly
After summer merrily.
Merrily, merrily shall I live now,
Under the blossom that hangs on the bough.

95 PROSPERO. Why, that's my dainty Ariel! I shall miss
thee,
But yet thou shalt have freedom. So, so, so.
To the King's ship, invisible as thou art;
There shalt thou find the mariners asleep
Under the hatches. The master and the boatswain
100 Being awake, enforce them to this place;
And presently, I prithee.

◄ What does Prospero ask Ariel to do?

ARIEL. I drink the air before me, and return
Or ere your pulse twice beat.   *Exit.*

GONZALO. All torment, trouble, wonder, and
amazement
105 Inhabits here. Some heavenly power guide us
Out of this fearful country!

PROSPERO.   Behold, sir King,
The wronged Duke of Milan, Prospero.
For more assurance that a living prince
Does now speak to thee, I embrace thy body,
110 And to thee and thy company I bid
A hearty welcome.

◄ In what way does Prospero describe himself? What reason does Prospero give for embracing Alonso?

ALONSO.   Whe'er thou beest he or no,[25]
Or some enchanted trifle[26] to abuse me
(As late I have been) I not know. Thy pulse
Beats as of flesh and blood; and since I saw thee,
115 The affliction of my mind amends, with which
I fear a madness held me. This must crave[27]
(And if this be at all) a most strange story.
Thy dukedom I resign, and do entreat
Thou pardon me my wrongs. But how should Prospero
120 Be living, and be here?

◄ What does Alonso say the unusual happenings on the island would make?

PROSPERO. [*To* GONZALO.] First, noble friend,
Let me embrace thine age, whose honor cannot

◄ What does Alonso say to Prospero about his lost dukedom?

---

24. **couch.** Lie
25. **Whe'er thou beest he or no.** Whether you are him or not
26. **enchanted trifle.** Magic trick
27. **crave.** Demand

Be measur'd or confin'd.

GONZALO.   Whether this be,
Or be not, I'll not swear.

PROSPERO.   You do yet taste
Some subtilties[28] o' th' isle, that will not let you
125 Believe things certain. Welcome, my friends all!
[*Aside to* SEBASTIAN *and* ANTONIO.] But you, my brace[29] of
        lords, were I so minded,[30]
I here could pluck his Highness' frown upon you
And justify[31] you traitors. At this time
I will tell no tales.

SEBASTIAN.   [*Aside.*] The devil speaks in him.

PROSPERO.   No.
130 For you, most wicked sir, whom to call brother
Would even infect my mouth, I do forgive
Thy rankest fault—all of them; and require
My dukedom of thee, which <u>perforce</u>, I know
Thou must restore.

ALONSO.   If thou beest Prospero,
135 Give us particulars of thy preservation,
How thou hast met us here, who three hours since
Were wrack'd upon this shore; where I have lost
(How sharp the point of this remembrance is!)
My dear son Ferdinand.

PROSPERO.   I am woe for't, sir.

140 ALONSO.   Irreparable is the loss, and patience
Says it is past her cure.

PROSPERO.   I rather think
You have not sought her help, of whose soft grace
For the like loss I have her <u>sovereign</u> aid,
And rest myself content.

ALONSO.   You the like loss!

▶ What are the "subtilties o' the isle"?

▶ With what does Prospero threaten Antonio and Sebastian?

▶ According to Prospero, why can't he call Antonio his brother? What does he forgive? What does he require? Does Antonio have any choice in the matter at hand?

▶ What does Prospero claim to have lost? In what way is he telling the truth?

---

28. **subtilties.** Illusions; visions
29. **brace.** Pair
30. **minded.** Of the mind to
31. **justify.** Show to be

Words
For
Everyday
Use

per • force (pər fôrs') *adv.,* by or through necessity
sov • er • eign (säv'rən) *adj.,* above or superior to all others

145 PROSPERO.   As great to me as late,[32] and, supportable
To make the dear loss, have I means much weaker
Than you may call to comfort you; for I
Have lost my daughter.

ALONSO.   A daughter?
O heavens, that they were living both in Naples,
150 The King and Queen there! That they were, I wish
Myself were mudded in that oozy bed
Where my son lies. When did you lose your daughter?

PROSPERO.   In this last tempest. I perceive these lords
At this encounter do so much admire
155 That they devour their reason, and scarce think
Their eyes do offices of truth,[33] their words
Are natural breath; but, howsoev'r you have
Been justled from your senses, know for certain
That I am Prospero, and that very duke
160 Which was thrust forth of Milan, who most strangely
Upon this shore (where you were wrack'd) was landed,
To be the lord on't. No more yet of this,
For 'tis a chronicle of day by day,
Not a relation for a breakfast, nor
165 Befitting this first meeting. Welcome, sir;
This cell's my court. Here have I few attendants,
And subjects none abroad: pray you, look in.
My dukedom since you have given me again,
I will requite you with as good a thing,
170 At least bring forth a wonder, to content ye
As much as me my dukedom.
Here PROSPERO *discovers* FERDINAND *and* MIRANDA *playing at
chess.*

MIRANDA.   Sweet lord, you play me false.[34]

FERDINAND.   No, my dearest
love,
I would not for the world.

MIRANDA.   Yes, for a score of kingdoms you should
wrangle,

◀ *For what does
Alonso wish?*

◀ *What will Prospero
give the nobles in
return for his restored
dukedom?*

◀ *What "wonder"
does Prospero reveal?*

---

32. **As great to me as late.** As great (a loss) to me as it is recent
33. **do offices of truth.** Accurately function
34. **play me false.** Lie or cheat

Words
For
Everyday
Use

jus • tle (jus'əl) *vt.*, bump or push, as in a crowd
wran • gle (raŋ´ gəl) *vi.*, argue or quarrel

175 And I would call it fair play.

ALONSO.   If this prove
A vision of the island, one dear son
Shall I twice lose.

SEBASTIAN.   A most high miracle!

FERDINAND.   Though the seas threaten, they are merciful;
I have cursed them without cause.   *Kneels.*

ALONSO.   Now all the blessings
180 Of a glad father compass[35] thee about!
Arise, and say how thou cam'st here.

MIRANDA.   O wonder!
How many goodly creatures are there here!
How beauteous mankind is! O brave new world
That has such people in't!

PROSPERO.   'Tis new to thee.

185 **ALONSO.**   What is this maid with whom thou wast at play?
Your eld'st acquaintance cannot be three hours.
Is she the goddess that hath sever'd us,
And brought us thus together?

FERDINAND.   Sir, she is mortal;
But by immortal Providence she's mine.
190 I chose her when I could not ask my father
For his advice, nor thought I had one. She
Is daughter to this famous Duke of Milan,
Of whom so often I have heard renown,
But never saw before; of whom I have
195 Receiv'd a second life; and second father
This lady makes him to me.

ALONSO.   I am hers.
But O, how oddly will it sound that I
Must ask my child forgiveness!

PROSPERO.   There, sir, stop.
Let us not burthen our remembrances with
200 A heaviness that's gone.

GONZALO.   I have inly wept,
Or should have spoke ere this. Look down, you gods,
And on this couple drop a blessed crown!
For it is you that have chalk'd[36] forth the way
Which brought us hither.

ALONSO.   I say, amen, Gonzalo!

What does Miranda think when she sees the group of assembled nobles? Are all the characters she is observing truly "goodly" and "beauteous"?

What does Alonso think about Miranda when he sees her for the first time?

What does Ferdinand say about Prospero?

What does Alonso mean by "I am hers"? What does he mean when he says that he must ask his child for forgiveness?

---

35. **compass.** Surround
36. **chalk'd.** Forged

205 GONZALO. Was Milan thrust from Milan, that his issue
Should become kings of Naples? O, rejoice
Beyond a common joy, and set it down
With gold on lasting pillars: in one voyage
Did Claribel her husband find at Tunis,

◄ What does
Gonzalo say has
been found on this
voyage?

210 And Ferdinand her brother, found a wife
Where he himself was lost; Prospero his dukedom
In a poor isle; and all of us, ourselves,
When no man was his own.

ALONSO.   [To FERDINAND and MIRANDA.] Give me
your hands.
Let grief and sorrow still embrace his heart
215 That³⁷ doth not wish you joy!

GONZALO.   Be it so, amen!

Enter ARIEL, with the MASTER and BOATSWAIN amazedly
following.

O, look, sir, look, sir! here is more of us.
I prophesied, if a gallows were on land,
This fellow could not drown. Now, blasphemy,³⁸
That swear'st grace o'erboard, not an oath on shore?³⁹
220 Hast thou no mouth by land? What is the news?

BOATSWAIN.   The best news is, that we have safely
found
Our king and company; the next, our ship—
Which, but three glasses⁴⁰ since, we gave out split—
Is tight and yare, and bravely rigg'd as when
225 We first put out to sea.

ARIEL.   [Aside to PROSPERO.] Sir, all this service
Have I done since I went.

PROSPERO.   [Aside to ARIEL.] My tricksy spirit!

ALONSO.   These are not natural events, they strengthen
From strange to stranger. Say, how came you hither?

◄ How does Alonso
feel when he hears
what the boatswain
reveals?

BOATSWAIN. If I did think, sir, I were well awake,
230 I'ld strive to tell you. We were dead of sleep,
And (how we know not) all clapp'd under hatches,
Where, but even now, with strange and several noises
Of roaring, shrieking, howling, jingling chains,
And moe diversity of sounds, all horrible,
235 We were awak'd; straightway, at liberty;
Where we, in all her trim, freshly beheld

---

37. **his heart / That.** The heart of anyone who
38. **blasphemy.** Person who blasphemes or curses
39. **That swear'st . . . shore.** You who throws heavenly grace overboard by your
cursing, why are you so quiet now?
40. **three glasses.** Three hours

Our royal, good, and gallant ship; our master
Cap'ring to eye her. On a trice, so please you,
Even in a dream, were we divided from them,
240 And were brought moping[41] hither.

ARIEL.   [*Aside to* PROSPERO.]   Was't well done?

PROSPERO.   [*Aside to* ARIEL.] Bravely, my diligence.
Thou shalt be free.

ALONSO.   This is as strange a maze as e'er men trod,
And there is in this business more than nature
245 Was ever conduct of. Some oracle
Must rectify our knowledge.

PROSPERO.   Sir, my liege,[42]
Do not infest[43] your mind with beating on
The strangeness of this business. At pick'd[44] leisure,
Which shall be shortly, single I'll resolve you
250 (Which to you shall seem probable) of every
These happen'd accidents; till when, be cheerful
And think of each thing well. [*Aside to* ARIEL.]   Come
    hither, spirit.
Set Caliban and his companions free;
Untie the spell.   [*Exit* ARIEL.]   How fares my gracious sir?
255 There are yet missing of your company
Some few odd lads that you remember not.

Enter ARIEL, *driving in* CALIBAN, STEPHANO AND TRINCULO, *in
their stol'n apparel.*

STEPHANO.   Every man shift for all the rest, and let no
man take care for himself; for all is but fortune.
Coraggio,[45] bully-monster, *coraggio!*

260 TRINCULO.   If these be true spies which I wear in my
    head, here's a goodly sight.

CALIBAN.   O Setebos, these be brave spirits indeed!
How fine my master is! I am afraid
He will chastise me.

SEBASTIAN.   Ha, ha!
265 What things are these, my lord Antonio?
Will money buy 'em?

ANTONIO.   Very like; one of them
Is a plain fish, and no doubt marketable.

---

41. **moping.** Disoriented
42. **liege.** Sovereign, lord
43. **infest.** Fill
44. **pick'd.** Convenient; easy
45. **Coraggio.** Courage

▶ Of what does
Prospero assure
Ariel?

▶ In what way does
Alonso describe all
the strange occur-
rences that are being
revealed?

▶ Who else used the
word brave to
describe the assem-
bled group of nobles?
Of what is Caliban
afraid?

PROSPERO.   Mark but the badges of these men, my lords,
Then say if they be true. This misshapen knave—
270 His mother was a witch, and one so strong
That could control the moon, make flows and <u>ebbs</u>,
And deal in her command without her power.
These three have robb'd me, and this demi-devil
(For he's a bastard one) had plotted with them
275 To take my life. Two of these fellows you
Must know and own, this thing of darkness I
Acknowledge mine.

◄ What does
Prospero acknowl-
edge as his own?

CALIBAN.   I shall be pinch'd to death.

ALONSO.   Is not this Stephano, my drunken butler?

SEBASTIAN.   He is drunk now. Where had he wine?

280 ALONSO.   And Trinculo is reeling ripe.[46] Where should
        they
Find this grand liquor that hath gilded[47] 'em?
How cam'st thou in this pickle?

TRINCULO.   I have been in such a pickle[48] since I saw
you last that I fear me will never out of my bones. I
285 shall not fear fly-blowing.[49]

SEBASTIAN.   Why, how now, Stephano!

STEPHANO.   O, touch me not, I am not Stephano, but a
        cramp.

PROSPERO.   You'ld be king o' the isle, sirrah?

STEPHANO.   I should have been a sore one then.

290 ALONSO.   This is a strange thing as e'er I look'd on.
                                    Pointing to CALIBAN.

PROSPERO.   He is as disproportion'd in his manners
As in his shape. Go, sirrah, to my cell;
Take with you your companions. As you look
To have my pardon, trim it handsomely.

◄ What does
Caliban promise?
What does he realize?

295 CALIBAN.   Ay, that I will; and I'll be wise hereafter,
And seek for grace. What a thrice-double ass

---

46. **reeling ripe.** Drunk
47. **gilded.** Flushed
48 **pickle.** Predicament
49. **fly-blowing.** Being infested by insects

Words
For
Everyday
Use   **ebb** (eb) *n.,* flow of water back toward the sea as the tide
             falls

Was I to take this drunkard for a god,
And worship this dull fool!

PROSPERO.   Go to, away!

ALONSO.   Hence, and bestow your luggage where you
found it.

300 SEBASTIAN.   Or stole it, rather.

Exeunt CALIBAN, STEPHANO, *and* TRINCULO.

PROSPERO.   Sir, I invite your Highness and your train
To my poor cell, where you shall take your rest
For this one night; which, part of it, I'll waste
With such <u>discourse</u> as, I not doubt, shall make it
305 Go quick away—the story of my life,
And the particular accidents gone by
Since I came to this isle. And in the morn
I'll bring you to your ship and so to Naples,
Where I have hope to see the nuptial[50]
310 Of these our dear-belov'd solemnized,
And thence retire me to my Milan, where
Every third thought shall be my grave.

ALONSO.   I long
To hear the story of your life, which must
Take the ear strangely.

PROSPERO.   I'll deliver all,
315 And promise you calm seas, auspicious gales,
And sail so <u>expeditious</u>, that shall catch
Your royal fleet far off.   [*Aside to* ARIEL.]   My Ariel,
chick,
That is thy charge. Then to the elements
Be free, and fare thou well!—Please you draw near.

Exeunt omnes.

► *What final com-mand does Prospero give to Ariel?*

---

50. **nuptial.** Wedding

Words For Everyday Use

dis • course (dis′kôrs′) *n.*, communication of ideas, informa-tion, etc.

ex • pe • di • tious (eks′pə dish′əs) *adj.*, efficient or speedy

Epilogue

Spoken by PROSPERO.

Now my charms are all o'erthrown,
And what strength I have's mine own,
Which is most faint. Now 'tis true,
I must be here confined by you,
5   Or sent to Naples. Let me not,
Since I have my dukedom got,
And pardon'd the deceiver, dwell
In this bare island by your spell,
But release me from my bands[1]
10   With the help of your good hands,
Gentle breath of yours my sails
Must fill, or else my project fails,
Which was to please. Now I want
Spirits to enforce, art to enchant,
15   And my ending is despair,
Unless I be relieved by prayer,
Which pierces so, that it assaults
Mercy itself, and frees all faults.
      As you from crimes would pardon'd be,
20   Let your indulgence set me free.

                                 Exit.

---

1. **bands.** Bonds

Responding to the Selection

If you were Prospero, would you "abjure" your "rough magic," break your staff, and drown your books of magic? Why, or why not?

Reviewing the Selection

Recalling and Interpreting

1. **R:** What does Ariel say would happen to Prospero if he saw the condition of the nobles? Does Prospero agree? According to Prospero, what is the nobler and "rarer action"?

2. **I:** In what way is Prospero's character changing in this act?

3. **R:** Which of his magical powers does Prospero describe in detail in his speech in act V, scene i, beginning with the line "Ye elves of hills, brooks, standing lakes, and groves"? What does he resolve to do in this speech?

4. **I:** What attitude does Prospero express toward his magic in the first part of this speech? in the latter part? Why does Prospero make this resolution? Explain whether Prospero has conflicting feelings about making this decision.

5. **R:** In act V, scene i, in the speech beginning with the line "A solemn air, and the best comforter," in what way does Prospero describe his brother Antonio? How does Prospero say he feels about Antonio's past actions? With what does Prospero later threaten Antonio and Sebastian in an aside? What would "infect" Prospero's mouth? What does Prospero require of Antonio? Does Antonio have a choice in this matter?

6. **I:** Does Prospero truly forgive his brother, or is he simply interested in regaining his dukedom? Why is the fact that Antonio remains silent in this act significant? Are the brothers reconciled? Explain.

7. **R:** What does Alonso restore to Prospero? According to Prospero, why does he embrace Alonso? What does Prospero say that he too has lost? For what does Alonso wish? What "wonder" does Prospero show Alonso to "content" him?

8. **I:** What does Prospero's embrace of Alonso represent? Why do you think Prospero continues to let Alonso believe that Ferdinand and Miranda are dead for a while? What is Prospero hoping to see in Alonso?

Synthesizing

9. In this act, Prospero says of Caliban, "this thing of darkness I / Acknowledge mine." This line has sometimes been interpreted to mean that Caliban represents Prospero's dark side and that Prospero is acknowledging this aspect of himself. Are Prospero and Caliban similar in any way, or are they completely different? What might Prospero's dark side be? Why might his acknowledgment and acceptance of this dark side be important? Explain whether or not you find this to be a reasonable interpretation of this line.

10. In the epilogue, to what is Shakespeare comparing a magician without his magic? Why is Prospero in a similar position to all the characters who have been held captive in the play? Sometimes the epilogue has been viewed as symbolizing Shakespeare's farewell to the theater. Others claim that this speech is simply a conventional means of appealing to the audience for applause. With which viewpoint do you agree, or do you have a different view of the epilogue? Support your response with your own reasoning as well as with examples from the text.

Understanding Literature (QUESTIONS FOR DISCUSSION)

1. **Classicism. Classicism** is a collection of ideas about literature and about art in general derived from the study of works by Greeks and Romans of the Classical Era. Dramas and works that emulate classical drama typically obey the unities of time and place. That is, the action of the drama takes place in one specific setting and during the time allotted for the play. *The Tempest* does follow this classical formula—the entirety of the play is set on the island, and the action all takes place within the space of a few hours. While Shakespeare's first comedy, *The Comedy of Errors,* obeyed the classical unities, many of his plays deviated widely from this form. Shakespeare frequently set a given play in many different locations and covered events over an expanse of years. Why do you think Shakespeare chose to follow the classical unities of place and time in this drama? What are the advantages and disadvantages of following the classical unities?

2. Resolution and Dénouement. The **resolution** is the point at which the central conflict, or struggle, is ended, or resolved. The **dénouement** is any material that follows the resolution and that ties up loose ends. In act V, Shakespeare seems to resolve the conflicts that have emerged during the play and to achieve reconciliation among his characters. Discuss whether all the troubling issues that have been raised throughout this drama are truly resolved, leaving no loose ends. How do you feel about the way in which the play is resolved? To focus your discussion, think about the following problems and issues: Prospero seeks penitence from those who have wronged him—Alonso, Antonio, and Caliban. Do all these characters express penitence? Is their penitence believable? Prospero says that he wants to show mercy and to forgive those who have wronged him. Does he do this? Whom does he forgive? Whom doesn't he truly forgive, and why? Has Prospero truly cast aside his vengeance? Why, or why not? Prospero says that he will not tell Alonso of Antonio and Sebastian's plot to take Alonso's life. Why might this decision adversely affect Alonso? Is Prospero aware of this? Is Prospero motivated by virtue and mercy or by the desire to regain his own political power? Why did Prospero choose Ferdinand as Miranda's future husband? How might this marriage further his goals? Does Prospero gladly renounce his powers? Why does he renounce his powers? What does Caliban realize? What does he promise? Do you think Caliban's change in character is heartfelt or motivated by fear of punishment? Discuss whether leaving troubling issues unresolved weakens or strengthens the play as a whole.

3. Symbol. A **symbol** is something that stands for or represents both itself and something else. Chess was a game primarily played by the nobly born, and it was associated with romantic partners. It is also a game that emulates a struggle between two opposing kingdoms. Why might Miranda and Ferdinand playing at chess be an appropriate symbol of reconciliation? In what way does the game comment upon the action of the play?

4. Irony and Dramatic Irony. **Irony** is a difference between appearance and reality. In **dramatic irony,** something is known by the reader or audience but unknown to the characters. When Miranda sees the group of assembled nobles, she remarks, "O, wonder! / How many goodly creatures are there here! / How beauteous mankind is! O brave new world, / That has such people in't!" Prospero dryly responds, "'Tis new to thee." What does Prospero mean?

Why does Prospero find Miranda's remark ironic? What do Prospero and the audience know that Miranda does not? These are Miranda's last lines in the play. Why are they typical of Miranda, given her character? In what way does Prospero's response comment on Miranda's character? on his own character? on the play in general?

Plot Analysis of *The Tempest*

The following diagram, known as Freytag's Pyramid, illustrates the main plot of *The Tempest*.

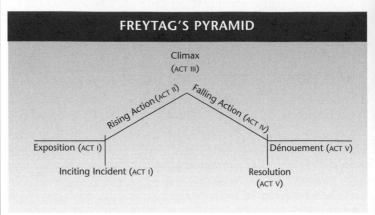

Exposition and Inciting Incident (Act I)

In a five-act play, the first act typically presents the setting and the main characters. The central conflict is also developed. In *The Tempest,* Prospero, with the aid of the spirit Ariel, raises a storm that strands a group of nobles, including Alonso, King of Naples; Sebastian, the king's brother; Ferdinand, the king's son; Gonzalo, a loyal counselor; and Antonio, Prospero's brother, on an island. Prospero has been living on this island with his daughter, Miranda, and a servant named Caliban, the son of a witch named Sycorax who formerly lived on the island. Prospero reveals to Miranda the play's central conflict: Prospero wishes to regain his dukedom, which was usurped by his brother, Antonio, with the aid of Alonso. Prospero was partially to blame for his own downfall, because he devoted all his time to study of the magical arts. A number of other conflicts are also introduced, such as the conflict between Prospero and Caliban, who resents serving Prospero; Ferdinand's separation from his father, whom he presumes to be dead; and Prospero's desire to form a match between Miranda and Ferdinand.

Rising Action (Act II)

In the second act of a five-act play, the central conflict is developed. In act II of *The Tempest,* the treachery described in act I continues as Antonio hatches a new scheme, convincing Sebastian to kill Alonso and claim the kingdom of

Naples. Another conflict is further developed when Caliban encounters Stephano and Trinculo and decides to make them his new masters to free himself from Prospero's service.

Climax (Act III)

The third act of a five-act play presents a decisive occurrence that determines the future course of events in the play. In act III of *The Tempest*, Miranda and Ferdinand admit their love for each other. Caliban convinces Stephano to kill Prospero and become king of the island, but Ariel, who is loyal to Prospero, overhears this scheme. While Prospero and Ariel look on, spirits offer a banquet to Alonso, Antonio, and Sebastian. Just as they are about to eat, Ariel appears as a harpy and makes the banquet disappear, saying the disappearance is a sign of their sin. Ariel also tells Alonso that Ferdinand is dead. Prospero strikes the three nobles with fits of madness, which Gonzalo interprets as a sign of their guilty consciences.

Falling Action (Act IV)

The fourth act of a five-act play presents events that happen as a result of the climax, or crisis. In act IV, Prospero offers Ferdinand Miranda's hand in marriage and puts on a masque, or a brief allegorical drama lavish in spectacle and performed by masked actors, to celebrate their love. Prospero and Ariel put a stop to Caliban, Stephano, and Trinculo's scheme.

Resolution and Dénouement (Act V)

The fifth act of a five-act play presents the event that resolves, or ends, the central conflict. It also ties up loose ends. In act V of *The Tempest,* Prospero relieves Alonso, Antonio, and Sebastian of their madness and reveals his identity to them. Alonso restores Prospero's dukedom to him. As recompense, Prospero reveals that his son Ferdinand is not dead at all but happily engaged to Miranda. Caliban says that he was wrong to plot against Prospero and says that he will behave differently in the future. Satisfied with regaining his lost dukedom, Prospero renounces his magic.

Creative Writing Activities

Creative Writing A: Narrative Pamphlet

As sources for *The Tempest,* Shakespeare may have used narrative pamphlets entitled *A Discovery of the Bermudas, Otherwise Called the Island of Devils; The True Estate of the Colony in Virginia;* and *True Reportory of the Wracke (Purchas His Pilgrims.)* These pamphlets reported the experiences of a group of mariners who ran aground on Bermuda, survived this wreck, and explored the island. Narrative pamphlets about explorers and seafarers who encountered strange new lands caused a sensation in Renaissance England and continued to remain popular for centuries. Pamphlets such as these were supposedly true accounts, but they often contained exaggerations and unrealistic descriptions. Write a narrative pamphlet about the island on which *The Tempest* takes place. You may write from the point of view of any of the members of the ship who were brought ashore by the tempest, or you might write from the point of view of Prospero himself. You should keep your chosen character in mind as you write the pamphlet and present that character's perceptions of the island. Rather than recounting the entire action of the play, your pamphlet should describe the island itself and its physical and magical qualities. You should, however, explain how your character ended up on the island, how he or she survived, and how he or she returned to civilization. Try to include vivid and exciting descriptions that would excite the imaginations of your audience. You may wish to satirize the titles of the pamphlets in your own title. For example, you might write *How Stephano, a Drunken Butler, Almost Became King of a Magical Island; The Wreck and Redemption of Alonso, King of Naples; Trinculo's Experiences with the Fishy Monster of the Magical Isle;* or *Prospero's True Account of the Subjugation of the Natives of the Isle to which He Was Unjustly Banished.*

Creative Writing B: A Dramatic Continuation

What might happen to the characters of *The Tempest* after the end of act V? What happens to Prospero, Alonso, Antonio, and Sebastian once they return to Italy? What happens to Ferdinand and Miranda? What happens to Ariel and Caliban? Are they left behind on the island, or do one or both of them return to Europe with Prospero? Does Prospero give up his magic for good? Choose a character, group of characters, or an issue in which you are interested, and write a brief, one- or two-scene dramatic continuation of *The Tempest.* Your continuation should be in proper dramatic form, using dialogue and stage directions instead of prose narration. You do not have to try to emulate Shakespeare's verse or language, but you may wish to try your hand at doing so in a line or two just for fun. Before beginning to write your dramatic continuation, freewrite about what you think should happen in your scene or scenes.

Creative Writing C: A Song

Renaissance audiences were fond of music and song. *The Tempest* is full of songs, but while characters such as Ariel, Caliban, Stephano, and the characters in the masque sing, others do not. Write a song for one of the characters who does not sing in *The Tempest.* For example, you might write a sad song for Alonso when he believes that his son is dead, a love song for Miranda or Ferdinand, a song about evil schemes for Antonio or Sebastian, or a song about mercy, forgiveness, and reconciliation for Prospero. Freewrite ideas for a song for one of *The Tempest*'s characters, and decide upon a definite mood for your song. Use a simple rhyme scheme such as *abab* or *aabb* when writing your song.

Creative Writing D: Persuasive Letter

Caliban says, "You taught me language, and my profit on't / Is, I know how to curse." Imagine that Caliban has a somewhat more positive view of language and decides to put what he has learned to use. Write a persuasive letter from Caliban to Prospero, explaining why Prospero's harsh treatment of him is unjust and offering reasons why Prospero should not treat him as a slave but as a valued friend and equal. Prospero is a scholarly person, so your arguments should be well thought out and should appeal to Prospero's reason and sense of mercy and justice. Remember that further offending Prospero would not be to Caliban's advantage, but state your case both convincingly and forcefully.

Critical Writing Activities

Critical Essay A: Analyzing Shakespeare's View of Nature and Civilization

Read Montaigne's essay "Of Cannibals," which appears in Selections for Additional Reading. Then, write an essay explaining in what way *The Tempest* can be seen as a response to Montaigne's view. Does Shakespeare agree that a "natural" society is superior to a "civilized" one? To begin your essay, first define Montaigne's view of "natural" and "civilized" societies. Then, examine how the theme of nature versus civilization and art is treated in *The Tempest* by freewriting your responses to the following questions and issues:

- Is Caliban a good example of an idealized "natural" person uncorrupted by the vices of civilization? What is Caliban's reaction to civilization? Has Caliban become corrupted by civilization, or is his inherent "nature" treacherous and brutal?
- Prospero educated both Miranda and Caliban in the solitude of this "natural" world. In what ways are their reactions to encountering the "civilized" world similar? In what ways are their reactions different? Given their similar upbringings, why did they turn out so differently? Is this difference the result of their inherent natures, or is it the result of the way in which Prospero "civilized" them?
- What does Shakespeare reveal about Renaissance attitudes toward native members of a natural society? about Renaissance attitudes toward disadvantaged members of their own society?
- Almost all the Europeans who come into contact with the island entertain the idea of becoming king or "lord on't." What happens when a member of the "civilized" world comes into contact with a "natural" world? What do the actions of "civilized" people reveal about them?
- What do all the plots to gain political power reveal about "civilized" people?
- Why do Antonio and Sebastian perceive the island differently than Gonzalo does? What does this reveal about the "nature" of these characters?
- What is the difference between art and civilization? What distinction is made in this play between art and language well used and art and language wrongly or scornfully used? What distinction is made between art and creative works and the empty works of courtly egotism and political maneuvering? Which characters represent the positive

aspects of civilization? Which characters represent the negative aspects of civilization?

After you have written down your thoughts about these questions, develop a thesis about Shakespeare's view of nature and civilization. In your first paragraph, clearly state both Montaigne's view and Shakespeare's view of nature and civilization, comparing and contrasting these views. You might organize your essay by devoting a paragraph to each of the bulleted questions and issues previously raised. Remember to refer to and quote from the text of *The Tempest* itself to support your ideas. Then come to a conclusion in a final paragraph.

Critical Essay B: Analyzing Caliban's Character

Modern interpreters sometimes view *The Tempest* as an early play about European exploration of the New World and the resulting colonization and exploitation of native peoples. These scholars tend to view Caliban very sympathetically and to see him as a victim. Renaissance audiences would have viewed Caliban very differently—as a comic figure and as somewhat of a villain. Caliban's past behavior toward Miranda and his brutal plot against Prospero would have been seen as acts typical of a villain. Do you agree with the Renaissance view of Caliban as a villain, do you agree with the modern view of Caliban as a victim, or do you see Caliban as a complex character who is neither a hapless victim nor a brutal villain? In other words, can you reconcile the sympathy of a modern audience for Caliban with the reaction of Shakespeare's contemporaries to his character? Write an essay explaining your view of Caliban's character. To begin, you might make a three-column chart. Label one column *Villain*, the second column *Victim*, and the third column *Caliban as Complex Character*. Then organize what the play reveals about Caliban into these columns. For example, under the column labeled *Villain*, you might write that Caliban says the only profit he has gained from language is that he knows how to curse, or that he is rejecting his education. In the second column labeled *Victim*, you might note that Caliban is rejecting the language of his oppressors. In the third column, you might note that despite the fact that Caliban claims to have rejected language, he speaks in poetry as often as in prose and that many of the passages attributed to him are filled with beautiful language and imagery. Refer to the details listed in your chart when formulating your thesis about Caliban's character. Support your thesis with evidence from the text, and come to a conclusion in a final paragraph.

Critical Essay C: Analyzing Theme

A **theme** is a central idea in a literary work. Shakespeare develops many themes in *The Tempest*. Choose one of the themes listed below, and write an essay in which you analyze Shakespeare's treatment of this theme and trace its development throughout the drama.

If you would like, you might choose more than one theme and explain the way in which these themes are related. To begin, freewrite your thoughts about your theme or themes.

Art and Magic	Reconciliation and Repentan
Freedom and Captivity	Transformation
Language	Treachery and Deception
Love	Nature and Civilization
Power	

Then, skim through *The Tempest,* keeping a list of passages in which your theme or themes are treated. After reviewing these passages and your freewriting, develop a thesis about your chosen theme or themes; support your thesis in following paragraphs using examples and quotations from the passages you listed; and come to a conclusion in a final paragraph.

Critical Essay D: Analyzing Miranda and Prospero's Relationship

In many of his plays, Shakespeare negatively portrays fathers who meddle in their children's decisions about whom to marry. In *The Tempest*, Shakespeare portrays Prospero, who is trying to arrange a marriage between Miranda and Ferdinand, more positively. Write an essay in which you explore Miranda and Prospero's relationship. To begin, freewrite answers to the following questions: How would you characterize this relationship? What decisions does Prospero make about Miranda's future? To what extent is he meddling in her choice of a future husband? To what extent is he allowing the love between Ferdinand and Miranda to blossom on its own? Why is Prospero interested in promoting this love? If Prospero is a meddler, why doesn't Shakespeare portray him more harshly? Is there a difference between the way in which Prospero tries to encourage love and the behavior of a father who orders his child to marry a chosen partner? After you have written about these questions, develop a thesis in which you describe the nature of Prospero and Miranda's relationship, and explain Prospero's role in Miranda and Ferdinand's relationship. Support your thesis with evidence from the text. Come to a conclusion about Shakespeare's attitude toward Prospero as a father in a final paragraph.

Projects

Project A: Designing Costumes and a Set

In Shakespeare's day, costumes were often the cast-off clothes of members of the nobility. For some productions, such as court masques, designers such as Inigo Jones created lavish costumes for sprites and fairies. Renaissance theaters were unlike modern proscenium or picture stages, which have three walls and a removed fourth wall. Elements of a Renaissance set were viewed from more than one angle. Today, productions vary from simple ones that present actors in jeans and T-shirts in bare-bones settings to elaborate ones employing all the skills of modern costume and set designers. Working in small groups, design costumes and a set for a production of *The Tempest*. Your group may choose to imagine that you are creating a set and costumes for a Renaissance audience. In this case, you might research Renaissance theater and dress as well as look at some of the costume designs done by Inigo Jones. As an alternative, your group might choose to create costumes and a set for a modern production of *The Tempest*. In this case, use your imagination to decide how elaborate or how simple a production you wish to stage. Your group should create color sketches of your set and costumes for the play's characters and share your creations with the rest of the class. In an oral presentation, your group should explain when your production is set and why you made the choices that you did.

Project B: Adapting a Court Masque

While court masques were popular during the Renaissance, this form of entertainment is unfamiliar to many modern readers and audiences. Working in small groups, brainstorm a list of ways in which you might adapt the masque in act IV to appeal to a modern audience. Once your group has come up with some good ideas, you should flesh out a plan for presenting act IV to a modern audience. For example, instead of having Ceres, Juno, and Iris appear to bless Ferdinand and Miranda's marriage, you might decide to have happily married couples appear to give Ferdinand and Miranda their recipes for successful marriage. Rather than including a rustic dance of reapers and nymphs, you might include the happily married couples waltzing. You might even decide to create an ultra-modern version of this act that would appeal to a younger audience. Your group should present your ideas to the class as well as show any drawings, sketches, or models that you have made.

Project C: Renaissance Attitudes towards the Other

Of the English, Trinculo says, "When they will not give a doit to relieve a lame beggar, they will lay out ten to see a dead Indian." Working in small groups, research the way Europeans of the Renaissance treated and reacted to the non-Europeans they encountered at the beginning of the Age of Exploration. Your group might wish to focus on the way the Spanish treated the Native Americans they encountered in the New World, the way the Portuguese treated the native Africans they encountered in West Africa, the way English colonists treated native peoples in the Virginia colony, the way English people viewed and treated native peoples who were brought back to England, European attitudes towards Moors (or those of Arabic descent), or even English attitudes toward another European people—those of Jewish descent. After researching your topic, your group should present its findings to the class.

Project D: Marriage in the Renaissance Period

While love as an ideal was valued during the Renaissance, many noble people still arranged marriages to further political goals, and many commoners married not for love but for economic reasons. With other classmates, form three groups. The first should research how the ideal of love evolved in Europe, focusing upon the development of courtly love in medieval times. The second should research famous marriages that were formed for political reasons in or before Shakespeare's time, as well as the reasons why Shakespeare's patron, Queen Elizabeth I, remained unmarried. The third group should research the conditions in which poor farmers and laborers lived and discuss why marriage may have been an economic necessity for such people. Each group should present its findings to the class.

Selections for Additional Reading

from *True Repertory of the Wracke (Purchas His Pilgrims)* by William Strachey

William Strachey (active from 1606 to 1618) was an English colonist whose letters relate some of the mishaps that befell the early European settlers of the New World. In 1607, the Virginia Company established the colony of Jamestown, Virginia. In 1609, four hundred new colonists set sail for Jamestown. The venture was filled with difficulties and disasters. At last, approaching the Virginia coast, the party faced a hurricane. In the storm, the governor's ship was separated from the rest of the fleet, driven by storms to the islands of Bermuda. Strachey's letter describes the storm, life on Bermuda, and the land of Virginia where the passengers eventually arrived. Strachey's letter was printed in 1625 but circulated in manuscript before that time. Most scholars agree that Shakespeare was familiar with Strachey's letter, but the impact of Strachey's letter and of similar reports on Shakespeare's writing of The Tempest *is still open to debate.*

A true repertory of the wreck and redemption of Sir Thomas Gates, Knight, upon and from the islands of the Bermudas, his coming to Virginia, and the estate of the colony then and after under the government of the Lord La Warre. July 15, 1610, written by William Strachey, Esquire.

A most dreadful tempest (the manifold deaths whereof are here to the life described), their wreck on Bermuda, and the description of those islands.

. . . We were within seven or eight days at the most . . . of making Cape Henry upon the coast of Virginia when on St. James his day, July 14, being Monday (preparing for no less all the black night before), the clouds gathering thick upon us, and the winds singing and whistling most unusually, which made us to cast off our pinnace (towing the same until then astern), a dreadful storm and hideous began to blow from out the northeast, which swelling and roaring as it were by fits, some hours with more violence than others, at length did beat all light from heaven, which like a hell of darkness turned black upon us, so much the more fuller of horror, as in such cases horror and fear use to overrun the troubled and overmastered senses of all, which, taken up with amazement, the ears lay so sensible to the terrible cries and murmurs of the winds and distraction of our company, as who was most armed and best prepared was not a little shaken. For surely . . . as death comes not so sudden nor apparent, so he comes not so elvish and painful (to men especially even then in health and perfect habitudes of body) as at sea; who comes at no time so welcome, but our frailty (so weak is the hold of hope in miserable demonstrations of danger) it makes guilty of many contrary changes and conflicts. For indeed, death is accompanied at no time nor place with circumstances everyway so uncapable of particularities of goodness and inward comforts as at sea. . . .

For four and twenty hours the storm in a restless tumult had blown so exceedingly as we could not apprehend in our imaginations any possibility of greater violence; yet did we still find it not only more terrible but more constant, fury added to fury, and one storm urging a second more outrageous than the former, whether it so wrought upon our fears, or indeed met with new forces. Sometimes strikes in our ship amongst women and passengers, not used to such hurly and discomforts, made us look one upon the other with troubled hearts and panting bosoms, our clamors drowned in the winds, and the winds in thunder. Prayers might well be in the heart and lips, but drowned in the outcries of the officers; nothing heard that could give comfort, nothing seen that might encourage hope. . . . Our sails wound up lay without their use, and if at any time we bore but a hullock, or half forecourse, to guide her before the sea, six and sometimes eight men were not enough to hold the whipstaff in the steerage and the tiller below in the gunner room, by which may be imagined the strength of the storm, in which the sea swelled above the clouds and gave battle to the heaven. It could not be said to rain; the waters like whole rivers did flood in the air. And this I did still observe, that whereas upon the land, when a storm hath poured itself forth once in drifts of rain, the wind as beaten down and vanquished therewith not long after endureth, here the glut of water, as if throttling the wind erewhile, was no sooner a little emptied and qualified but instantly the winds, as having gotten their mouths now free and at liberty, spake more loud and grew more tumultuous and malignant. What shall I say? Winds and seas were as mad as fury and rage could make them. For mine own part, I had been in some storms before, . . . yet all that I had ever suffered gathered together might not hold in comparison with this: there was not a moment in which the sudden splitting or instant oversetting of the ship was not expected.

Howbeit this was not all; it pleased God to bring a greater

affliction yet upon us, for in the beginning of the storm we had received likewise a mighty leak. . . .

And the ship in every joint almost, having spewed out her oakam, before we were aware (a casualty more desperate than any other that a voyage by sea draws with it) was grown five foot suddenly deep with water above her ballast, and we almost drowned within, while we sat looking when to perish from above. This imparting no less terror than danger, ran through the whole ship with much fright and amazement, startled and turned the blood, and took down the bravery of the most hearty mariner of them all, insomuch as he that before happily felt not the sorrow of others, now began to sorrow for himself, when he saw such a pond of water so suddenly broken in, and which he knew could not (without present avoiding) but instantly sink him. . . The Lord knows, I had as little hope, as desire of life in the storm, and in this, it went beyond my will; because beyond my reason, why we should labor to preserve life; yet we did, either because so dear are a few lingring hours of life in all mankind, or that our Christian knowledge taught us, how much we owed to the rights of nature, as bound, not to be false to ourselves, or to neglect the means of our own preservation; the most despairful things amongst men, being matters of no wonder nor moment with him, who is the rich fountain and admirable essence of all mercy. . . .

Our governor, upon the Tuesday morning (at what time, by such who had been below in the hold, the leak was first discovered), had caused the whole company, about one hundred and forty, besides women, to be equally divided into three parts, and opening the ship in three places (under the forecastle, in the waist, and hard by the bittacle) appointed each man where to attend; and thereunto every man came duly upon his watch, took the bucket or pump for one hour, and rested another. Then men might be seen to labour, I may well say, for life, and the better sort, even our governor and admiral themselves, not refusing their turn and to spell each the other, to give example to other. The common sort stripped naked, as men in galleys, the easier both to hold out and to shrink from under the salt water, which continually leapt in among them, kept their eyes waking and their thoughts and hands working, with tired bodies and wasted spirits, three days and four nights destitute of outward comfort, and desperate of any deliverance, testifying how mutually willing they were yet by labor to keep each other from drowning, albeit each one drowned whilst he labored.

Once so huge a sea broke upon the poop and quarter

upon us as it covered our ship from stern to stem like a garment or a vast cloud; it filled her brimful for a while within, from the hatches up to the spardeck. This source or confluence of water was so violent as it rushed and carried the helmsman from the helm and wrested the whipstaff out of his hand, which so flew from side to side that when he would have ceased the same again, it so tossed him from starboard to larboard as it was God's mercy it had not split him. It so beat him from his hold and so bruised him as a fresh man hazarding in by chance fell fair with it, and by main strength bearing somewhat up made good his place, and with much clamor encouraged and called upon others, who gave her now up, rent in pieces and absolutely lost. Our governor was at this time below at the capstan, both by his speech and authority heartening every man unto his labor. It struck him from the place where he sat, and groveled him and all us about him on our faces, beating together with our breaths all thoughts from our bosoms else than that we were now sinking. For my part, I thought her already in the bottom of the sea; and I have heard him say wading out of the flood thereof, all his ambition was but to climb up above hatches to die *in aperto coelo*, and in the company of his old friends. . . .

During all this time the heavens looked so black upon us that it was not possible the elevation of the pole might be observed, nor a star by night nor sunbeam by day was to be seen. Only upon the Thursday night Sir George Summers being upon the watch had an apparition of a little round light, like a faint star, trembling and streaming along with a sparkling blaze half the height upon the mainmast, and shooting sometimes from shroud to shroud, 'tempting to settle as it were upon any of the four shrouds; and for three or four hours together, or rather more, half the night it kept with us, running sometimes along the mainyard to the very end and then returning. At which Sir George Summers called divers about him and showed them the same, who observed it with much wonder and carefulness; but upon a sudden, towards the morning watch, they lost the sight of it, and knew not what way it made. The superstitious seamen make many constructions of this sea-fire, which nevertheless is usual in storms: the same, it may be, which the Grecians were wont in the Mediterranean to call Castor and Pollux, of which if only one appeared without the other, they took it for an evil sign of great tempest. The Italians and such who lie open to the Adriatic and Tyrrhene Sea call it a sacred body, *corpo sancto*; the Spaniards call it Saint Elmo, and have an authentic and miraculous legend for it. Be it what it will, we laid other foundations of safety or ruin than in the rising or falling of it; could it have served us now miraculously to have taken our height by, it might have strucken amazement and a reverence in our devotions, according to the due of a miracle. But it did not light us any whit the more to our known way, who ran now (as do hoodwinked men) at all adventures, sometimes north and northeast, then north and by west, and in an instant again varying two or three points, and sometimes half the compass. East and by south we steered away as much as we could to bear upright, which was no small carefulness nor pain to do, albeit we much unrigged our ship, threw overboard much luggage, many a trunk and chest (in which I suffered no mean loss) and staved many a butt of beer, hogsheads of oil, cider, wine, and vinegar, and heaved away all our ordnance on the starboard side, and had now purposed to have cut down the mainmast the more to lighten her; for we were much spent, and our men so weary as their strengths together failed them with their hearts, having travailed now from Tuesday till Friday morning, day and night, without either sleep or food; for the leakage taking up all the hold, we could neither come by beer nor fresh water; fire we could keep none in the cookroom to dress any meat; and carefulness, grief, and our turn at the pump or bucket were sufficient to hold sleep from our eyes . . . and from Tuesday noon till Friday noon we bailed and pumped two thousand ton, and yet do what we could, when our ship held least in her (after Tuesday night second watch) she bore ten foot deep, at which stay our extreme working had kept her one eight glasses, forbearance whereof had instantly sunk us, and it being now Friday, the fourth morning, it wanted little but that there had been a general determination to have shut up hatches and, commending our sinful souls to God, committed the ship to the mercy of the sea; surely that night we must have done it, and that night had we then perished. But see the goodness and sweet introduction of better hope by our merciful God given unto us. Sir George Summers, when no man dreamed of such happiness, had discovered and cried land. Indeed, the morning now three-quarters spent had won a little clearness from the days before, and it being better surveyed, the very trees were seen to move with the wind upon the shore side; whereupon our governor commanded the helmsman to bear up, the boatswain sounding at the first found it thirteen fathom, and when we stood a little in, seven fathom, and presently heaving his lead the third time had ground at four fathom; and by this we had got her within a mile under the southeast point of the land, where we had somewhat smooth water. But having no hope to save her by coming to an anchor in the same, we were enforced to run her ashore as near the land as we could, which brought us within three-quarters of a mile of shore, and by the mercy of God unto us, making out our boats, we had ere night brought all our men, women, and children, about the number of one hundred and fifty, safe into the island.

We found it to be the dangerous and dreaded island, or rather islands, of the Bermuda, whereof let me give your ladyship a brief description before I proceed to my narration. And that the rather, because they be so terrible to all that ever touched on them, and such tempests, thunders, and other fearful objects are seen and heard about them that they may be called commonly the Devil's Islands, and are feared and avoided of all sea travelers alive, above any other place in the world. Yet it pleased our merciful God to make even this hideous and hated place both the place of our safety and means of our deliverance.

And hereby also I hope to deliver the world from a foul and general error, it being counted of most that they can be no habitation for men, but rather given over to devils and wicked spirits; whereas indeed we find them now by experience to be as habitable and commodious as most countries of the same climate and situation, insomuch as if the entrance into them were as easy as the place itself is contenting, it had long ere this been inhabited as well as other islands. Thus shall we make it appear that Truth is the daughter of Time, and that men ought not to deny everything which is not subject to their own sense.

The Bermudas be broken islands, five hundred of them in manner of an archipelagus (at least if you may call them all islands that lie, how little soever, into the sea, and by themselves), of small compass, some larger yet than other, as time and the sea hath won from them and eaten his passage through, and all now lying in the figure of a croissant within the circuit of six or seven leagues at the most, albeit at first it is said of them that they were thirteen or fourteen leagues, and more in longitude, as I have heard.

These islands are often afflicted and rent with tempests, great strokes of thunder, lightning, and rain in the extremity of violence. . . .

The soil of the whole island is one and the same, the mold dark, red, sandy, dry, and uncapable, I believe, of any of our commodities or fruits. Sir George Summers in the beginning of August squared out a garden . . . and sowed muskmelons, peas, onions, radish, lettuce, and many English seeds and kitchen herbs. All which in some ten days did appear above ground, but whether by the small birds, of which there were many kinds, or by flies (worms I never saw any, nor any venomous thing, as toad or snake or any creeping beast hurtful, only some spiders, which as many affirm are signs of great store of gold; but they were long and slender-leg spiders, and whether venomous or no I know not—I believe not, since we should still find them amongst our linen in our chests and drinking cans, but we never received any danger from them; a kind of melolontha, or black beetle, there was, which bruised, gave a savor like many sweet and strong gums pounded together)—whether, I say, hindered by these or by the condition or vice of the soil, they came to no proof, nor thrived. It is like enough that the commodities of the other western islands would prosper there, as vines, lemons, oranges, and sugar canes: our governor made trial of the latter and buried some two or three in the garden mold, which were reserved in the wreck amongst many which we carried to plant here in Virginia, and they began to grow; but the hogs breaking in both rooted them up and ate them. There is not through the whole islands either champaign ground, valleys, or fresh rivers. They are full of shaws of goodly cedar, fairer than ours here of Virginia, the berries whereof our men seething, straining, and letting stand some three or four days made a kind of pleasant drink. . . .

Likewise there grow great store of palm trees, not the right Indian palms, such as . . . are called cocos . . . nor of those kind of palms which bears dates, but a kind of cimarrons or wild palms in growth, fashion, leaves and branches, resembling those true palms; for the tree is high and straight, sappy and spongeous, unfirm for any use; no branches but in the uppermost part thereof, and in the top grow leaves about the head of it (the most inmost part whereof they call palmeto, and it is the heart and pith of the same trunk, so white and thin as it will peel off into pleats as smooth and delicate as white satin, into twenty folds, in which a man may write as in paper) where they spread and fall downward about the tree like an overblown rose or saffron flower not early gathered; so broad are the leaves as an Italian umbrella: a man may well defend his whole body under one of them from the greatest storm rain that falls. . . .

Sure it is that there are no rivers nor running springs of fresh water to be found upon any of them. When we came first we digged and found certain gushings and soft bubblings, which being either in bottoms or on the side of hanging ground were only fed with rain water, which nevertheless soon sinketh into the earth and vanisheth away, or emptieth itself out of sight into the sea, without any channel above or upon the superficies of the earth; for according as their rains fell, we had our wells and pits (which we digged) either half full or absolute exhausted and dry, howbeit some low bottoms (which the continual descent from the hills filled full, and in those flats could have no passage away) we found to continue as fishing ponds or standing pools continually, summer and winter, full of fresh water.

The shore and bays round about when we landed first afforded great store of fish, and that of divers kinds, and good. . . . We have taken also from under the broken rocks crayfish often greater than any of our best English lobsters, and likewise abundance of crabs, oysters, and whelks. . . .

Fowl there is in great store, small birds, sparrows fat and plump like a bunting, bigger than ours, robins of divers colours, green and yellow, ordinary and familiar in our cabins, and other of less sort. White and grey hernshaws, bitterns, teal, snipes, crows, and hawks, of which in March we found divers aeries, goshawks, and tercels; oxen-birds, cormorants, bald coots, moorhens, owls, and bats in great store. . . . A kind of webfooted fowl there is, of the bigness of an English green plover, or sea-mew, which all the summer we saw not, and in the darkest nights of November and December (for in the night they only feed) they would come forth, but not fly far from home, and hovering in the air and over the sea made a strange hollow and harsh howling. . . . Our men found a pretty way to take them, which was by standing on the rocks or sands by the seaside and holloing, laughing and making the strangest outcry that possibly they could, with the noise whereof the birds would come flocking to that place and settle upon the very arms and head of him that so cried, and still creep nearer and nearer, answering the noise themselves, by which our men would weigh them with their hand, and which weighed heaviest they took for the best and let the others alone, and so our men would take twenty dozen in two hours of the chiefest of them; and they were a good and well-relished fowl, fat and full as a partridge. . . .

We had knowledge that there were wild hogs upon the island, at first by our own swine preserved from the wreck and brought to shore; for they straying into the woods, an huge wild boar followed down to our quarter, which at night was watched and taken . . . and there be thousands of them in the islands, and at that time of the year, in August, September, October, and November they were well fed with berries that dropped from the cedars and the palms, and in our quarter we made sties for them. . . .

The tortoise is reasonable toothsome (some say) whole-some meat. I am sure our company liked the meat of them very well, and one tortoise would go further amongst them than three hogs. One turtle (for so we called them) feasted well a dozen messes, appointing six to every mess. It is such a kind of meat as a man can neither absolutely call fish nor flesh, keeping most what in the water, and feeding upon sea grass like a heifer in the bottom of the coves and bays, and laying their eggs (of which we should find five hundred at a time in the opening of a she turtle) in the sand by the shore side, and so covering them close leave them to the hatching of the sun. . . . Their eggs are as big as geese eggs, and them-selves grown to perfection, bigger than great round targets.

[Trouble arises among the settlers. A conspiracy is discov-ered and stopped.]

In these dangers and devilish disquiets (whilst the almighty God wrought for us and sent us, miraculously delivered from the calamities of the sea, all blessings upon the shore to content and bind us to gratefulness) thus enraged amongst ourselves to the destruction of each other, into what a mischief and misery had we been given up had we not had a governor with his authority to have suppressed the same? Yet was there a worse practice, faction and conju-ration afoot, deadly and bloody, in which the life of our gov-ernor, with many others, were threatened, and could not but miscarry in his fall. But such is ever the will of God (who in the execution of his judgments breaks the firebrands upon the head of him who first kindles them), there were who conceived that our governor indeed neither durst nor had authority to put in execution or pass the act of justice upon anyone, how treacherous or impious soever; their own opin-ions so much deceiving them for the unlawfulness of any act which they would execute, daring to justify among them-selves that if they should be apprehended before the perfor-mance, they should happily suffer as martyrs. They perse-vered therefore not only to draw unto them such a number and associates as they could work in to the abandoning of our governor and to the inhabiting of this island. They had now purposed to have made a surprise of the storehouse and to have forced from thence what was therein, either of meal, cloth, cables, arms, sails, oars, or what else it pleased God that we had recovered from the wreck and was to serve our general necessity and use, either for the relief of us while we stayed here, or for the carrying of us from this place again when our pinnace should have been furnished.

But as all giddy and lawless attempts have always something of imperfection, and that as well by the property of the action, which holdeth of disobedience and rebellion (both full of fear), as through the ignorance of the devisers themselves, so in this, besides those defects, there were some of the association who, not strong enough fortified in their own conceits, broke from the plot itself, and before the time was ripe for the execution thereof discovered the whole order and every agent and actor thereof, who nevertheless were not suddenly apprehended, by reason the confederates were divided and separated in place, some with us, and the chief with Sir George Summers in his island (and indeed all his whole company); but good watch passed upon them, every man from thenceforth commanded to wear his weapon, without which, before, we freely walked from quarter to quarter and conversed among ourselves; and every man advised to stand upon his guard, his own life not being in safety, whilst his next neighbour was not to be trusted. The sentinels and nightwarders doubled, the passages of both the quarters were carefully observed, by which means nothing was further attempted until a gentleman amongst them, one Henry Paine, the thirteenth of March, full of mischief, and every hour preparing something or other, stealing swords, adzes, axes, hatchets, saws, augurs, planes, mallets, etc. to make good his own bad end, his watch night coming about, and being called by the captain of the same to be upon the guard, did not only give his said commander evil language, but struck at him, doubled his blows, and when he was not suffered to close with him, went off the guard, scoffing at the double diligence and attendance of the watch appointed by the governor for much purpose, as he said; upon which the watch telling him if the governor should understand of his insolency, it might turn him to much blame, and haply be as much as his life were worth. The said Paine replied with a settled and bitter violence and in such unreverent terms as I should offend the modest ear too much to express it in his own phrase, but the contents were how the governor had no authority of that quality to justify upon anyone how mean soever in the colony an action of that nature, and therefore let the governor (said he) kiss etc. Which words being with the omitted additions brought the next day unto every common and public discourse, at length they were delivered over to the governor, who, . . . calling the said Paine before him, and the whole company, where (being soon convinced both by the witness of the commander and many which were upon the watch with him) our governor, who had now the eyes of the whole colony fixed upon him, condemned him to be instantly hanged; and the ladder being ready, after he had made many confessions, he earnestly desired, being a gentleman, that he might be shot to death; and towards the evening he had his desire, the sun and his life setting together.

But for the other which were with Sir George, upon the Sunday following . . . by a mutual consent forsook their labor and Sir George Summers, and like outlaws betook them to the wild woods. Whether mere rage, and greediness after some little pearl (as it was thought) wherewith they conceived they should forever enrich themselves, and saw how to obtain the same easily in this place, or whether the desire forever to inhabit here, or whatever other secret else moved them thereunto, true it is, they sent an audacious and formal petition to our governor subscribed with all their names and seals, not only entreating him that they might stay here, but with great art importuned him that he would perform other conditions with them, and not wave nor evade from some of his own promises, as namely to furnish each of them with two suits of apparel and contribute meal rateably for one whole year, so much among them as they had weekly now, which was one pound and a half a week, for such had been our proportion for nine months. Our governor answered this their petition, writing to Sir George Summers to this effect.

[The petition is granted. Two people stay in Bermuda, while the rest of the company sails to Virginia. Strachey describes their pleasure in the land. The settlers find that Jamestown is not well governed.]

What England may boast of, having the fair hand of husbandry to manure and dress it, God and nature have favourably bestowed upon this country, and as it hath given unto it both by situation, height, and soil all those (past hopes) assurances which follow our well-planted native country, and others lying under the same influence, if, as ours, the country and soil might be improved and drawn forth, so hath it endowed it, as is most certain, with many more, which England fetches far unto her from elsewhere. For first we have experience, and even our eyes witness (how young soever we are to the country) that no country yields goodlier corn nor more manifold increase; large fields we have, as prospects of the same, and not far from our palisado. Besides, we have thousands of goodly vines in every hedge and bosk running along the ground, which yield a plentiful grape in their kind. Let me appeal then to knowledge, if these natural vines were planted, dressed, and ordered by skilful vignerons whether we might not make a perfect grape and fruitful vintage in short time? And we have made trial of our own English seeds, kitchen herbs, and roots, and find them to prosper as speedily as in England.

[Strachey quotes from the Virginia Company's pamphlet *A True Declaration of Virginia.*]

The ground of all those miseries was the permissive providence of God, who, in the forementioned violent storm separated the head from the body, all the vital powers of regiment being exiled with Sir Thomas Gates in those infortunate (yet fortunate) islands. The broken remainder of those supplies made a greater shipwreck in the continent of Virginia by the tempest of dissension; every man overvaluing his own worth would be a commander, every man underprizing another's value denied to be commanded.

The next fountain of woes was secure negligence and improvidence, when every man sharked for his present booty, but was altogether careless of succeeding penury. Now I demand whether Sicilia or Sardinia, sometimes the barns of Rome, could hope for increase without manuring? A colony is therefore denominated because they should be *coloni*, the tillers of the earth and stewards of fertility; our mutinous loiterers would not sow with providence, and therefore they reaped the fruits of too dear-bought repentance. An incredible example of their idleness is the report of Sir Thomas Gates, who affirms that after his first coming thither he hath seen some of them eat their fish raw, rather than they would go a stone's cast to fetch wood and dress it. *Dii laboribus omnia vendunt*, God sells us all things for our labor, when Adam himself might not live in paradise without dressing the garden.

from "Of Cannibals"
by Michel de Montaigne, translated by John Florio

*Michel Eyquem de Montaigne (1533–1592) was a French writer who helped to shape the form of nonfiction writing known as the essay. An **essay** is a brief work of prose nonfiction. The original meaning of the term essay was "a trial or attempt." Montaigne published three books of essays in which he tentatively explored various subjects.*

In 1562, Montaigne met three natives of Brazil who had been brought back to France by the explorer Nicolas Durand de Villegagnon. This meeting and his readings of the reports of several travelers to the New World led him to write "Of Cannibals." In this essay, Montaigne argues that the inhabitants of the New World, seen as barbarous by Europeans, were more humane, more natural, and in many other ways superior to Europeans. With a tolerance of other cultures that differs greatly from the views commonly held by his contemporaries, Montaigne offers sharp criticism of the horrors attributed to his fellow Europeans. This translation from the French was made by John Florio in 1603. While Shakespeare probably did not have a source for the action of The Tempest, *the theme of the play does show the influence of Montaigne's famous essay.*

Now (to return to my purpose) I find, as far as I have been informed, there is nothing in that nation that is either barbarous or savage, unless men call that barbarism which is not common to them. As indeed we have no other aim of truth and reason than the example and idea of the opinions and customs of the country we live in. Where is ever perfect religion, perfect policy, perfect and complete use of all things. They are even savage as we call those fruits wild which nature of herself and of her ordinary progress has produced, whereas indeed they are those which ourselves have altered by our artificial devices and diverted from their common order we should rather term savage. In those are the true and most profitable virtues and natural proprieties most lively and vigorous which in these we have bastardized, applying them to the pleasure of our corrupted taste. And if, notwithstanding, in divers fruits of those countries that were never tilled we shall find that in respect of ours they are most excellent and as delicate unto our taste, there is no reason art should gain the point of honor of our great and puissant mother Nature. We have so much by our inventions surcharged the beauties and riches of her works that we have altogether overchoked her; yet wherever her purity shines, she makes our vain and frivolous enterprises wonderfully ashamed.

> *Et veniunt hederae sponte sua melius, Surgit*
> *et in solis formosior arbutus antris,*
> *Et volucres nulla dulcius arte canunt.*
> Ivies spring better of their own accord,
> Unhaunted plots much fairer trees afford,
> Birds by no art much sweeter notes record.
> —Propertius

All our endeavours or wit cannot so much as reach to represent the nest of the least birdlet, its contexture, beauty, profit, and use, no, nor the web of a silly spider. All things, says Plato, are produced either by nature, by fortune, or by art. The greatest and fairest by one or other of the two first, the least and imperfect by the last. Those nations seem therefore so barbarous unto me because they have received very little fashion from human wit, and are yet near their original naturality. The laws of nature do yet command them, which are but little bastardized by ours. And that with such purity as I am sometimes grieved the knowledge of it came no sooner to light at what time there were men that better than we could have judged of it. I am sorry Lycurgus and Plato had it not, for meseemes that what in those nations we see by experience does not only exceed all the pictures wherewith licentious poesy has proudly embellished the golden age and all her quaint inventions to feign a happy condition of man, but also the conception and desire of philosophy. They could not imagine a genuity so pure and simple as we see it by experience, nor ever believe our society might be maintained with so little art and human combination. It is a nation, would I answer Plato, that has no kind of traffic, no knowledge of letters, no intelligence of numbers, no name of magistrate nor of politic superiority, no use of service, of riches or of poverty, no contracts, no successions, no dividences, no occupation but idle, no respect of kindred but common, no apparel but natural, no manuring of lands, no use of wine, corn, or metal. The very words that import lying, falsehood, treason, dissimulation, covetousness, envy, detraction, and pardon were never heard of amongst them. How dissonant would he find his imaginary commonwealth from this perfection?

> *Hos natura modos primum dedit.*
> Nature at first uprise
> These manners did devise.
> —Virgil

Furthermore, they live in a country of so exceeding pleasant and temperate situation that, as my testimonies have further assured me, they never saw any man there either shaking with the palsy, toothless, with eyes dropping, or crooked and stooping through age. They are seated alongst the seacoast, encompassed toward the land with huge and steepy mountains, having between both a hundred leagues or thereabouts of open and champaign ground. They have great abundance of fish and flesh that have no resemblance at all with ours, and eat them without any sauces or skill of cookery, but plain boiled or broiled. The first man that brought a horse hither, although he had in many other voyages conversed with them, bred so great a horror in the land that before they could take notice of him, they slew him with arrows. Their buildings are very long, and able to contain two or three hundred souls, covered with barks of great trees, fastened in the ground at one end, interlaced and joined close together by the tops after the manner of some of our granges, the covering whereof hangs down to the ground and steads them as a flank. They have a kind of wood so hard that, riving and cleaving the same, they make blades, swords, and gridirons to broil their meat with. Their beds are of a kind of cotton cloth fastened to the house roof, as our ship cabins; everyone has his several couch, for the women lie from their husbands. They rise with the sun and feed for all day as soon as they are up, and make no more meals after that. They drink not at meat, as Suidas reports of some other people of the east which drank after meals, but drink many times a day, and are much given to pledge carouses. Their drink is made of a certain root, and of the color of our claret wines, which lasts but two or three days; they drink it warm. It has somewhat a sharp taste, wholesome for the stomach, nothing heady, but laxative for such as are not used unto it, yet very pleasing to such as are accustomed unto it. Instead of bread they use a certain white composition like unto corianders confected. I have eaten some, the taste whereof is somewhat sweet and wallowish. They spend the whole day in dancing. Their young men go a-hunting after wild beasts with bows and arrows. Their women busy themselves therewhilst with warming of their drink, which is their chiefest office. Some of their old men, in the morning before they go to eating, preach in common to all the household, walking from one end of the house to the other, repeating one self-same sentence many times till he have ended his turn (for their buildings are a hundred paces in length), he commends but two things unto his auditory: first, valor against their enemies, then lovingness unto their wives. They never miss, for their restraint, to put men in mind of this duty, that it is their wives which keep their drink luke-warm and well-seasoned. The form of their beds, cords, swords, blades, and wooden bracelets wherewith they cover their handwrists when they fight, and great canes open at one end by the sound of which they keep time and cadence in their dancing, are in many places to be seen, and namely in mine own house. They are shaven all over, much more close and cleaner than we are, with no other razors than of wood or stone. They believe their souls to be eternal, and those that have deserved well of their gods to be placed in that part of heaven where the sun rises, and the cursed toward the west in opposition. They have certain prophets and priests which commonly abide in the mountains and very seldom show themselves unto the people; but when they come down, there is a great feast prepared and a solemn assembly of many townships together (each grange as I have described makes a village, and they are about a French league one from another). The prophet speaks to the people in pub-lic, exhorting them to embrace virtue and follow their duty. All their moral discipline contains but these two articles: first, an undismayed resolution to war; then an inviolable affection to their wives. He does also prognosticate of things to come and what success they shall hope for in their enter-prises; he either persuades or dissuades them from war; but if he chance to miss of his divination, and that it succeed oth-erwise than he foretold them, if he be taken, he is hewn in a thousand pieces and condemned for a false prophet. And therefore he that has once misreckoned himself is never seen again. Divination is the gift of God, the abusing whereof should be a punishable imposture. When the divines amongst the Scythians had foretold an untruth, they were couched along upon hurdles full of heath or brushwood, and so manacled hand and foot, burned to death. Those which manage matters subject to the conduct of man's sufficiency are excusable, although they show the utmost of their skill. But those that gull and cony-catch us with the assurance of an extraordinary faculty, and which is beyond our knowl-edge, ought to be double punished, first because they per-form not the effect of their promise, then for the rashness of their imposture and unadvisedness of their fraud. They war against the nations that lie beyond their mountains, to which they go naked, having no other weapons than bows or wooden swords sharp at one end, as our broaches are. It is an admirable thing to see the constant resolution of their combats, which never end but by effusion of blood and murder, for they know not what fear or routs are. Every victor brings home the head of the enemy he has slain as a trophy of his victory and fastens the same at the entrance of his dwelling place. After they have long time used and entreated their prisoners well and with all commodities they can devise, he that is the master of them, summoning a great assembly of his acquaintance, ties a cord to one of the prisoners' arms, by the end whereof he holds him fast, with some distance from him for fear he might offend him, and gives the other arm bound in like manner to the dearest friend he has, and both in the presence of all the assembly kill him with swords; which done, they roast and then eat him in common, and send some slices of him to such of their friends as are absent. It is not, as some imagine, to nourish themselves with it (as anciently the Scythians wont to do), but to represent an extreme and inexpiable revenge. Which we prove thus: some of them perceiving the Portugals, who had confederated themselves with their adversaries, to use another kind of death when they took them as prisoners, which was to bury them up to the middle and against the upper part of the body to shoot arrows, and then, being almost dead, to hang them up, they supposed that these people of the other world (as they who had sowed the knowledge of many vices amongst their neighbours and were much more cunning in all kinds of evils and mischief than they) undertook not this manner of revenge without cause, and that consequently it was more smartful and cruel than theirs, and thereupon began to leave their old fashion to follow this. I am not sorry we note the barbarous horror of such an action, but grieved that prying so narrowly into their faults we are so blinded in ours. I think there is more barbarism in eating men alive than to feed on them being dead; to mangle by tortures and torments a body full of lively sense, to roast him in pieces, to make dogs and swine to gnaw and tear him in mammocks (as we have not only read, but seen very lately, yea, and in our own memory, not amongst ancient enemies, but our neighbours and fellow citizens, and—which is worse—under pretence of piety and religion), than to roast and tear him after he is dead. Chrysippus and Zeno, arch pillars of the Stoic sect, have supposed that it was no hurt at all, in time of need, and to what end soever, to make use of our carrion bodies and to feed upon them as did our forefathers, who, being besieged by Caesar in the city of Alexia, resolved to sustain the famine of the siege with the bodies of old men, women, and other persons unserviceable and unfit to fight.

Vascones (fama est) alimentis talibus usi
Produxere animas.
Gascons (as fame reports)
Lived with meats of such sorts.
—Juvenal

And physicians fear not, in all kinds of compositions availful to our health, to make use of it, be it for outward or inward applications; but there was never any opinion found so unnatural and immodest that would excuse treason, treachery, disloyalty, tyranny, cruelty, and such like, which are our ordinary faults. We may then well call them barbarous in regard of reason's rules, but not in respect of us that exceed them in all kind of barbarism.

from "The Story of Jason and Medea"
  from *Metamorphoses*
by Ovid (Publius Ovidius Naso), translated by Arthur Golding

Ovid was a classical Roman poet whose work was much admired in Shakespeare's time. Metamorphoses *is perhaps Ovid's greatest work. It is a vast compendium of the myths of classical Greece and Rome, many of which deal with miraculous transformations. Shakespeare modeled the character of the witch Sycorax on the character of Medea portrayed in* Metamorphoses. *Medea was a magician who had the gift of prophecy, but she sometimes used her magic to achieve wicked ends. While Shakespeare distinguishes Prospero's "art" from black magic, Prospero does echo some of Medea's lines from the* Metamorphoses *in act V, scene i, in the speech beginning "Ye elves of hills, brooks, standing lakes and groves." While Shakespeare could read Ovid's work in the original Latin, he was probably influenced by this poetic translation made by Arthur Golding in 1567.*

Ye Ayres and windes: ye Elves of Hilles, of Bookes, of
     Woods alone,
Of standing Lakes, and of the Night approche ye
     everychone.
Through helpe of whom (the crooked bankes much won-
     dring at the thing)
I have compelled streames to run cleane backward to their
     spring.
By charmes I make the calme Seas rough, and make the
     rough seas plain
And cover all the Skie with Cloudes, and chase them
     thence againe.
By charmes I rayse and lay the windes, and burst the
     Vipers jaw,
And from the bowels of the Earth both stones and trees
     doe drawe.
Whole woods and Forestes I remove: I make the
     Mountaines shake,
And even the Earth it selfe to grone and fearfully to quake.
I call up dead men from their graves: and thee O light-
     some Moone
I darken oft, though beaten brasse abate thy perill soone.
Our Sorcerie dimmes the Morning faire, and darkes the
     Sun at Noone.

Glossary

PRONUNCIATION KEY

VOWEL SOUNDS

a	hat	ō	go	ʉ	burn
ā	play	ô	paw, born	ə	extra
ä	star	o͝o	book, put		under
e	then	o͞o	blue, stew		civil
ē	me	oi	boy		honor
i	sit	ou	wow		bogus
ī	my	u	up		

CONSONANT SOUNDS

b	but	l	lip	t	sit
ch	watch	m	money	th	with
d	do	n	on	v	valley
f	fudge	ŋ	song, sink	w	work
g	go	p	pop	y	yell
h	hot	r	rod	z	pleasure
j	jump	s	see		
k	brick	sh	she		

A

a • bysm (ə biz´əm) *n.*, abyss

al • lay (a lā´) *vt.*, calm

ap • per • tain • ing (ap´ər tān´iŋ) *adj.*, relating to

as • per • sion (ə spʉr´zhən) *n.*, sprinkling of water, as in baptism

aus • pi • cious (ôs pish´ əs) *adj.*, favorable

aus • tere • ly (ôs stir´lē) *adv.*, harshly

B

boun • te • ous (boun´ tē əs) *adj.*, giving freely and generously without restraint

bri • er (brī´ər) *n.*, any prickly or thorny bush

C

cell (sel) *n.*, small room or cubicle

con • ten • tious (kən ten´shəs) *adj.*, argumentative

cred • u • lous (krej´o͞o ləs) *adj.*, easily convinced

D

dis • course (dis´ kôrs´) *n.*, communication of ideas, information, etc.

E

ebb (eb) *n.,* flow of water back toward the sea as the tide falls

en • mi • ty (en′mə tē) *n.,* hostility

en • sue (en so͞o′) *vi.,* come afterward; follow immediately

ex • pe • di • tious (eks′pə dish′əs) *adj.,* efficient or speedy

ex • tir • pate (ek′stər pāt′) *vt.,* destroy

G

gait (gāt) *n.,* manner of moving on foot

gar • ner (gär′nər) *n.,* place for storing

I

in • cite (in sīt′) *vt.,* set into motion, urge

in • dig • na • tion (in′dig nā′shən) *n.,* anger or scorn

in • fir • mi • ty (in fur′mə tē) *n.,* feebleness, weakness

im • por • tuned (im′pôr to͞on′d) *vt.,* asked for urgently; demanded of

in • vert (in vurt′) *vt.,* turn upside down

in • vet • er • ate (in vet′ər it) *adj.,* firmly established

J

jus • tle (jus′əl) *vt.,* bump or push, as in a crowd

M

ma • lig • nant (mə lig′nənt) *adj.,* having evil influence; harmful

man • a • cle (man′ə kəl) *vt.,* restrain by tying or chaining up

mu • ti • neer (myo͞ot′′n ir′) *n.,* person guilty of revolting against his or her officers (especially on a ship)

P

par • a • gon (par′ə gän′) *n.,* model of perfection or excellence

pen • i • tent (pen′i tənt) *adj.,* truly sorry for having sinned and willing to atone

per • di • tion (pər dish′ən) *n.,* loss, ruin

per • fid • i • ous (pər fid′ē əs) *adj.,* treacherous; faithless

per • force (pər fôrs′) *adv.,* by or through necessity

pre • rog • a • tive (prē räg′ə tiv) *n.,* right or privilege

pres • ci • ence (presh′əns) *n.,* foreknowledge

pur • pos • ed (pur′pəs′d) *vt.,* intended

R

rat • i • fy (rat′ə fī′) *vt.,* confirm

re • pose (ri pōz´) *vt.*, lie at rest

re • pose (ri pōz´) *n.*, rest; peace

rev • el (rev'əl) *n.*, festive merrymaking

S

sin • ew (sin'yo͞o) *n.*, tendon; source of power or strength

sov • er • eign (säv'rən) *adj.*, above or superior to all others

sov • er • eign • ty (säv´rən tē) *n.*, sovereign state or governmental unit

sup • plant (sə plant´) *vt.*, remove by force

U

un • mit • i • ga • ble (un mit´ə gə´bəl) *adj.*, absolute; unstoppable

u • surp (yo͞o zʉrp´) *vt.*, take or assume power by force

V

val • iant (val´yənt) *adj.*, brave

W

wran • gle (raŋ´gəl) *vi.*, argue or quarrel

Handbook of Literary Terms

Allegory. An **allegory** is a work in which each element *symbolizes*, or represents, something else. In *naive allegory*, characters, objects, places, and actions personify abstractions. In more sophisticated allegories, elements of the work make up an *extended metaphor* in which the elements are described but their part-by-part interpretation is left up to the reader.

Anagram. An **anagram** is a word or a phrase created by rearranging the letters of another word or phrase. The title of Samuel Butler's novel *Erewhon* is an anagram for *nowhere*.

Aside. An **aside** is a statement made by a character in a play, intended to be heard by the audience but not by other characters on the stage.

Character. A **character** is a person (or sometimes an animal) who figures in the action of a literary work. A *protagonist,* or *main character,* is the central figure in a literary work. An *antagonist* is a character who is pitted against a protagonist. *Major characters* play significant roles in a work. *Minor characters* play lesser roles. A *one-dimensional character, flat character,* or *caricature* is one who exhibits a single dominant quality, or *character trait.* A *three-dimensional, full,* or *rounded character* is one who exhibits the complexity of traits associated with actual human beings. A *static character* does not change during the course of the action. A *dynamic character* does change. A *stock character* is one found again and again in different literary works.

Classicism. **Classicism** is a collection of ideas about literature and about art in general derived from the study of works by Greeks and Romans of the Classical Era. Definitions of what constitutes the Classical style differ, but most would agree that the Classical aesthetic emphasizes authority, austerity, clarity, conservatism, decorum, imitation, moderation, order, reason, restraint, self-control, simplicity, tradition, and unity.

Comedy. Originally a literary work with a happy ending, a **comedy** is any lighthearted or humorous work, especially one prepared for the stage or the screen. Comedy is often contrasted with tragedy, in which the hero meets an unhappy fate. (It is perhaps only a slight exaggeration to say that comedies end with wedding bells and tragedies with funeral bells.) Comedies typically present less-than-exalted characters who display all-too-human limitations, foibles, faults, and misunderstandings. The typical progression of the action in a comedy is from initial order to a humorous misunderstanding or confusion and back to order again. Stock elements of comedy include mistaken identity, word play, satire, and exaggerated characters and events.

Conflict. A **conflict** is a struggle between two forces in a literary work. A *plot* involves the introduction, development, and eventual resolution of a conflict. One side of the *central conflict* in a story or drama is usually taken by the *main character.* That character may struggle against another character, against the forces of nature, against society or social norms, against fate, or against some element within himself or herself. A struggle that takes place between a character and some outside force is called an *external conflict.* A struggle that takes place within a character is called an *internal conflict.*

Dénouement. See *plot.*

Dramatic irony. See *irony.*

Foil. A **foil** is a character whose attributes, or characteristics, contrast with and therefore throw into relief the attributes of another character. In Shakespeare's *Hamlet,* for example, Fortinbras, a determined, self-assured person of action, provides a foil for Hamlet, who is plagued with doubts and cannot commit himself to a course of action.

Iamb. An **iamb** is a poetic foot containing one weakly stressed syllable followed by one strongly stressed syllable, as in the words *afraid* and *release.* A line of poetry made up of iambs is said to be *iambic.*

Iambic. See *iamb.*

Irony. **Irony** is a difference between appearance and reality. Types of irony include the following: *dramatic irony,* in which something is known by the reader or audience but unknown to the characters; *verbal irony,* in which a statement is made that implies its opposite; and *irony of situation,* in which an event occurs that violates the expectations of the characters, the reader, or the audience.

Metaphor. A **metaphor** is a figure of speech in which one thing is spoken or written about as if it were another. This figure of speech invites the reader to make a comparison between the two things. The two "things" involved are the writer's actual subject, the *tenor* of the metaphor, and another thing to which the subject is likened, the *vehicle* of the metaphor. When, in Meditation 17, John Donne writes that "all mankind is of one author and is one volume," he is using two metaphors:

TENOR	VEHICLE
mankind	a volume or book
God	the author of the volume or book

Similes are a type of metaphor. See *simile.*

Meter. The **meter** of a poem is its rhythmical pattern. English verse is generally described as being made up of rhythmical units called *feet,* as follows:

TYPE OF FOOT	STRESS PATTERN	EXAMPLE
iambic	⏑ /	insist
trochaic	/ ⏑	freedom
anapestic	⏑ ⏑ /	unimpressed
dactylic	/ ⏑ ⏑	feverish
spondaic	/ /	baseball

Some scholars also use the term *pyrrhic* to describe a foot with two weak stresses. Using this term, the word *unbelievable* might be described as consisting of two feet, an anapest followed by a pyrrhic:

$$⏑ \quad ⏑ \quad / \quad | \quad ⏑ \quad ⏑$$
$$\text{un} \quad \text{be} \quad \text{liev} \quad | \quad \text{a} \quad \text{ble}$$

Terms used to describe the number of feet in a line include the following: *monometer* for a one-foot line; *dimeter* for a two-foot line; *trimeter* for a three-foot line; *tetrameter* for a four-foot line; *pentameter* for a five-foot line; *hexameter,* or *Alexandrine,* for a six-foot line; *heptameter* for a seven-foot line; *octameter* for an eight-foot line.

A seven-foot line of iambic feet is called a *fourteener.*

A complete description of the meter of a line includes both the term for the type of foot that predominates in the line and the term for the number of feet in the line. The most common English meters are iambic tetrameter and iambic pentameter. The following are examples of each:

IAMBIC TETRAMETER:

$$⏑ \quad / \quad ⏑ \quad / \quad ⏑ \quad / \quad ⏑ \quad /$$
$$\text{O slow} \quad | \quad \text{ly, slow} \quad | \quad \text{ly rose} \quad | \quad \text{she up}$$

IAMBIC PENTAMETER:

$$⏑ \quad / \quad ⏑ \quad / \quad ⏑ \quad / \quad ⏑ \quad / \quad ⏑ \quad /$$
$$\text{The cur} \quad | \quad \text{few tolls} \quad | \quad \text{the knell} \quad | \quad \text{of part} \quad | \quad \text{ing day}$$

Parallelism. Parallelism is a rhetorical technique in which a writer emphasizes the equal value or weight of two or more ideas by expressing them in the same grammatical form. William Blake uses parallelism in these lines from "The Lamb":

And I made a rural pen,
And I stain'd the water clear,
And I wrote my happy songs
Every child may joy to hear.

Plot. A **plot** is a series of events related to a central *conflict*, or struggle. A typical plot involves the introduction of a conflict, its development, and its eventual resolution. Terms used to describe elements of plot include the following:

- The **exposition**, or **introduction**, sets the tone or mood, introduces the characters and the setting, and provides necessary background information.
- The **inciting incident** is the event that introduces the central conflict.
- The **rising action**, or **complication**, develops the conflict to a high point of intensity.
- The **climax** is the high point of interest or suspense in the plot.
- The **crisis**, or **turning point**, often the same event as the climax, is the point in the plot where something decisive happens to determine the future course of events and the eventual working out of the conflict.
- The **falling action** is all of the events that follow the climax.
- The **resolution** is the point at which the central conflict is ended, or resolved.
- The **dénouement** is any material that follows the resolution and that ties up loose ends.
- The **catastrophe**, in tragedy, is the event that marks the ultimate tragic fall of the central character. Often this event is the character's death.

Plots rarely contain all these elements in precisely this order. Elements of exposition may be introduced at any time in the course of a work. A work may begin with a catastrophe and then use flashback to explain it. The exposition, or dénouement, or even the resolution may be missing. The inciting incident may occur before the beginning of the action actually described in the work. These are but a few of the many possible variations that plots can exhibit. See *conflict*.

Prose. **Prose** is the broad term used to describe all writing that is not drama or poetry, including fiction and nonfiction. Types of prose writing include novels, short stories, essays, and journalism. Most biographies, autobiographies, and letters are written in prose. See *fiction*.

Scene. A **scene** is a short section of a literary work that presents action that occurs in a single place or at a single time. Long divisions of dramas are often divided into scenes.

Setting. The **setting** of a literary work is the time and place in which it occurs, together with all the details used to create a sense of a particular time and place. Writers create setting by various means. In fiction, setting is most often revealed by description of such elements as landscape, scenery, buildings, furniture, clothing, the weather, and the season. It can also be revealed by how characters talk and behave. In its widest sense, setting includes the general social, political, moral, and psychological conditions in which characters find themselves.

Spectacle. In drama, the **spectacle** is all the elements that are presented to the senses of the audience, including the lights, setting, costumes, makeup, music, sound effects, and movements of the actors.

Stage directions. **Stage directions** are notes included in a play, in addition to the dialogue, for the purpose of describing how something should be performed on stage. Stage directions describe setting, lighting, music, sound effects, entrances and exits, properties, and the movements of characters. They are usually printed in italics and enclosed in brackets or parentheses.

Simile. A **simile** is a comparison using *like* or *as*.

Symbol. A **symbol** is a thing that stands for or represents both itself and something else. Writers use two types of symbols—conventional and personal or idiosyncratic. A *conventional symbol* is one with traditional, widely recognized associations. Such symbols include doves for peace; laurel wreaths for heroism or poetic excellence; the color green for jealousy; the color purple for royalty; the color red for anger; morning or spring for youth; winter, evening, or night for old age; wind for change or inspiration; rainbows for hope; roses for beauty; the moon for fickleness or inconstancy; roads or paths for the journey through life; woods or darkness for moral or spiritual confusion; thorns for troubles or pain; stars for unchangeableness or constancy; mirrors for vanity or introspection; snakes for evil or duplicity; and owls for wisdom. A *personal* or *idiosyncratic symbol* is one that assumes its secondary meaning because of the special use to which it is put by a writer.

Theme. A **theme** is a central idea in a literary work.

Tone. **Tone** is the emotional attitude toward the reader or toward the subject implied by a literary work. Examples of the different tones that a work may have include familiar, ironic, playful, sarcastic, serious, and sincere.